THE EUCHARISTIC MIRACLES OF THE WORLD

By the Institute of St. Clement I, Pope and Martyr

In cooperation with the *Pontifical Academy Cultorum Martyrum* and the
Real Presence Eucharistic Education and Adoration Association

Original title:
I Miracoli Eucaristici nel mondo. Catalogo della mostra internazionale.

Published in the United States of America by
Eternal Life
Bardstown, KY

THE EUCHARISTIC MIRACLES OF THE WORLD
By the Institute of St. Clement I, Pope and Martyr
In cooperation with the *Pontifical Academy Cultorum Martyrum* and the
Real Presence Eucharistic Education and Adoration Association

Original title:
I Miracoli Eucaristici nel mondo. Catalogo della mostra internazionale.
©The Institute of St. Clement I, Pope and Martyr

©2009 Real Presence Eucharistic Education and Adoration Association
(www.therealpresence.org)

ISBN 978-1-931101-02-8

January 2009
Published in the United States of America by

E   L

Eternal Life ®
902 W. Stephen Foster Avenue
Bardstown, KY 40004
1-800-842-2871
www.lifeeternal.org

Acknowledgments

We thank young Carlo Acutis, who died at the age of 15, whose Cause of Beatification has been opened by the Diocese of Milan (www.carloacutis.com). It was Carlo who first had the idea of producing the exhibition and who helped to realize its fulfillment.

Due to the promoter of this exhibition, Monsignor Rafaello Martinelli of the St. Ambrose and St. Charles Basilica (an official of the Congregation for the Doctrine of the Faith and member of the editorial commission of the Compendium of the Catechism of the Catholic Church), and the kind willingness of Antonia Salzano Acutis of the Pontifical Academy Cultorum Martyrum, this photographic Eucharistic miracles exhibition is made possible. With an extensive assortment of photographs and historical descriptions, the exhibition, sponsored by the Institute of St. Clement I, Pope and Martyr, presents some of the principal Eucharistic miracles that took place throughout the ages in various countries of the world, and have been recognized by the Church.

In love and honor to the Sacred Heart of Jesus we would like to thank His Excellency, the Most Reverend Raymond L. Burke, Archbishop Emeritus of St. Louis (now serving, as appointed by His Holiness Benedict XVI in June 2008, as Prefect of the Supreme Tribunal of the Apostolic Signatura), for his unwavering spiritual leadership in shepherding us into the New Evangelization through a continuous endeavor to promote devotion to the Real Presence of Jesus Christ in the Blessed Sacrament by means of Eucharistic adoration and education.

We give special thanks to Reverend Burns K. Seeley, S.S.J.C., Ph.D., St. John Cantius, Chicago, Illinois, for his spiritual guidance and expert hands-on direction which have made the Vatican International Exhibition possible. May Father Seeley (R.I.P. October 4, 2007) rest in Eternal Beatitude.

We acknowledge the extraordinary efforts of Reverend Gino Dalpiaz, C.S., whose invaluable expertise was so generously offered. In addition to translating stories of the Eucharistic miracles, Father translated the Italian introductions, the book covers and various other tasks in helping to bring this project to a successful completion. Our gratitude would not be complete without thanking Rev. Eugene C. Morris, S.T.L., for making the overall check of the material presented.

We especially want to thank each of the individual translators (Italian into English) who volunteered their skills and time in order to bring the *Eucharistic Miracles of the World* exhibition to the people of the United States of America. May these narratives of Church-approved Eucharistic miracles bring a greater understanding and appreciation of what the unbloody Sacrifice of the Mass gives us: the Real Presence of Jesus Christ, Body and Blood, Soul and Divinity, in the Most Holy Eucharist.

Maria De Rosa-Bellahcen, Translator, B.A. Italian Language and Literature, University of Notre Dame, Munster, Indiana

Daniel Campbell, Pasadena, California

Rev. Gino Dalpiaz, C.S., Scalabrini House of Theology, Chicago, Illinois

Lisa Lucafo D'Ambrosio, B.A. Italian Language and Literature, Loyola University, Chicago, Illinois

Lillian Santoro-Davis, National Centre for Padre Pio, Inc., Barto, Pennsylvania

Rev. Msgr. Robert J. Dempsey, Pastor, St. Philip the Apostle Parish, Northfield, Illinois

Fr. Simeon Distefano, OFM, Immaculate Conception Province, New York City, New York

Wiley Feinstein, Professor of Italian, Loyola University, Chicago, Illinois

Lucia Ferruzzi, Loyola University, Chicago, Illinois

Michael Gibson, Munster, Indiana

Reverend John Griffiths, J.C.D., Archdiocese of Chicago, Illinois

John Michael A. Kunz, Ph.L., Doctoral Candidate in Philosophy at the Università Pontificio della Santa Croce in Rome, Italy, La Palma, California

Maria Labriola, Italian Instructor, Lewis University, Romeoville, Illinois

Rev. Christopher A. Layden, S.T.L., Peoria, Illinois

Ada Locatelli, Fr. Kolbe Missionaries of the Immaculata, West Covina, California

Omar Loggiodice, Mount St. Mary's Seminary, Emmitsburg, Maryland

Cav. (Cavaliere della Republica Italiana) Antonio Lombardo, Editor of *Il Pensiero*, St. Louis, Missouri

Rev. J.C.M., C.S., New York, New York

Rev. Mario Malacrida, M.C.C.J., Comboni Missionaries Theologate, Chicago, Illinois

Mariella Michelon, Italian Instructor, Dominican University, Triton College, Forest Park, Illinois

Elizabeth A. Mitchell, Ph.D., Director of Development, Trinity Academy, Pewaukee, Wisconsin

Father Thomas A. Milota, S.T.L., Sacred Heart Parish, Lombard, Illinois

John Norton, Monrovia, California

Ronald J. Rychlak, University of Mississippi, School of Law, Oxford, Mississippi

Father Aniello Salicone, Xaverian Missionary, St. Therese Chinese Mission, Chicago, Illinois

Rev. Frederick Sucher, C.P., Congregation of the Passion: Immaculate Conception Community, Chicago, Illinois

Our utmost gratitude goes to Eternal Life and St. Martin's Printshop for their continued generous and steadfast support in promoting the Real Presence of Jesus Christ in the Holy Eucharist from which the "Church draws her life" for the transformation of the world, which is the goal of the New Evangelization.

Table of Contents

Our Lady of the Eucharist

Miraculous Communions

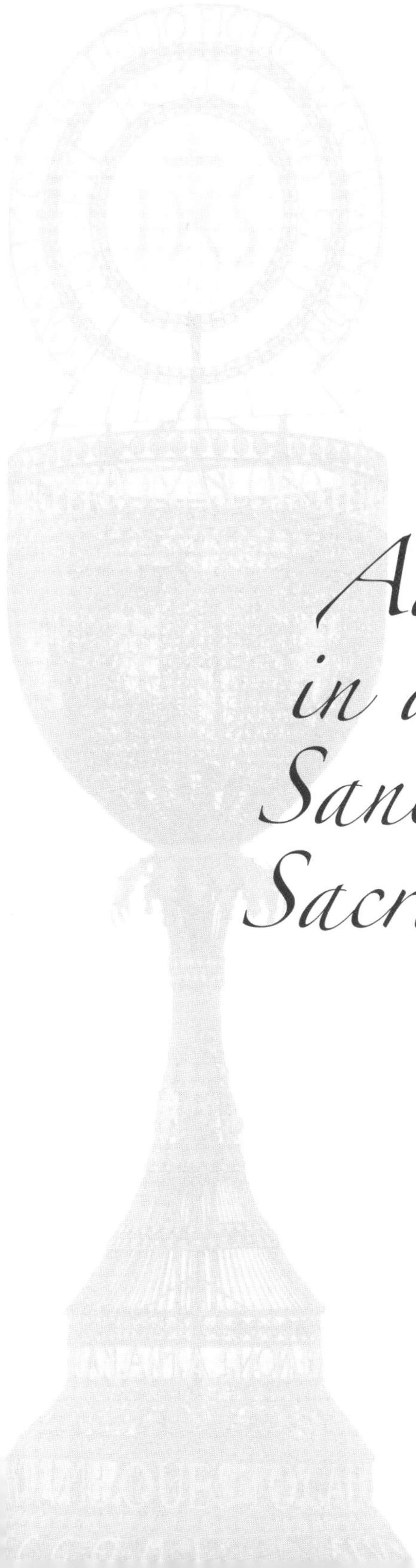

*Adoremus
in aeternum
Sanctissimum
Sacramentum.*

Foreword

Our late and most beloved Pope John Paul II called us repeatedly to take up the work of the New Evangelization, that is, to bring Christ to a totally secularized world by teaching, celebrating and living our Catholic faith as if for the first time. He constantly directed us to the Blessed Virgin Mary and to the saints, also of our own time, as examples of the holiness of life to which the New Evangelization calls us for the salvation of our souls and the transformation of our world, and as friends and intercessors in meeting the many challenges of leading a holy life. He urged us to be one with our Blessed Mother and the whole communion of saints in looking upon the Face of Christ, in hearing His invitation to put out into the deep (*Lk* 5:4), and in putting aside our doubts and fears in order to bring Him to the world.

The last three major documents of Pope John Paul II's pontificate form a unity in presenting to us the program of the New Evangelization and in urging us to embrace it with the enthusiasm and energy of the first disciples and the first missionaries to our continent and nation. They are the Apostolic Letter *Novo millennio ineunte,* "At the Close of the Great Jubilee of the Year 2000" (January 6, 2001); the Apostolic Letter *Rosarium Virginis Mariae,* "On the Most Holy Rosary" (October 16, 2002); and the Encyclical Letter *Ecclesia de Eucharistia,* "On the Eucharist in Its Relationship to the Church" (April 17, 2003—Holy Thursday).

The goal of the New Evangelization is, as Pope John Paul II explains in the Encyclical Letter *Ecclesia de Eucharistia,* "to rekindle" our loving wonder before the Holy Eucharist, the great Mystery of Faith. Let us read again his words to us:

> I would like to rekindle this Eucharistic "amazement" by the present Encyclical Letter, in continuity with the Jubilee heritage which I have left to the Church in the Apostolic Letter *Novo millennio ineunte* and its Marian crowning, *Rosarium Virginis Mariae.* To contemplate the Face of Christ, and to contemplate it with Mary, is the "program" which I have set before the Church at the dawn of the Third Millennium, summoning her to put out into the deep on the sea of history with the enthusiasm of the New Evangelization. To contemplate Christ involves being able to recognize Him wherever He manifests Himself, in His many forms of presence, but above all in the living sacrament of His Body and His Blood. *The Church draws her life from Christ in the Eucharist*; by Him she is fed and by Him she is enlightened (*Ecclesia de Eucharistia*, n. 6).

The Holy Eucharist is the source at which Christ's life is nourished within us with the incomparable Food which is His Body, Blood, Soul and Divinity. The Holy Eucharist is the highest expression of our life in Christ, for it unites us sacramentally to Christ in the Sacrifice of the Cross, which is made always new in the celebration of the Holy Mass.

In the last years of his pontificate, our late and beloved Pontiff directed his attention, above all else, to teaching us about the Holy Eucharist and to restoring the discipline by which the Holy Mass is celebrated and the Holy Eucharist is reposed in the tabernacle and worshiped outside of the Holy Mass. In the final year of his service as Vicar of Christ, he called us to observe the Year of the Eucharist (October 2004 to October 2005). The Year of the Eucharist began with the International Eucharistic Congress held at Guadalajara in Mexico, and concluded with the Ordinary Assembly of the Synod Bishops, "The Eucharist: Source and Summit of the Life and the Mission of the Church," at which Pope John Paul II's successor, Pope Benedict XVI, presided.

As we carry forward the work of the New Evangelization, the Eucharistic Mystery is the source of our direction and strength. At the same time, the deeper knowledge and love of the Holy Eucharist, born of our loving wonder and "amazement" at the mystery of God's love for us in His Son, Jesus Christ, is our goal. To assist us in reawakening and deepening our love of the Holy Eucharist, The Real Presence Association, an apostolate founded by the late Father John A. Hardon, S.J., tireless apostle and catechist of the Eucharist, has worked with the Pontifical Academy *Cultorum Martyrum* (founded to promote and deepen the veneration of the Holy Martyrs), to present, in English, the story of 126 miracles associated with faith in and worship of the Most Blessed Sacrament. Each of the miracles is venerated at a shrine, all of which have been approved by the Diocesan Bishop and some of which have the approval of the Holy See. Cooperating with the Pontifical Academy, the Real Presence Association has made available in English the Vatican International Exhibition, *The Eucharistic Miracles of the World*.

The miracles presented in the Vatican International Exhibition, like all miracles, are gifts from God "to witness to some truth or to testify to someone's sanctity" (Father John A. Hardon, S.J., *Modern Catholic Dictionary*, p. 352). It should not surprise us that God has granted so many miracles to deepen our knowledge and love of His greatest gift to us, the gift of the Body and Blood of His only-begotten Son, our Lord Jesus Christ, as the Heavenly Food of our earthly pilgrimage and the Medicine of eternal life.

The Eucharistic Miracles of the World provides a wonderful service to the work of the New Evangelization. The popular devotion associated with each miracle is a most worthy vehicle of the New Evangelization. As Pope Paul VI taught us in his *Magna Carta* on the New Evangelization, the Apostolic Exhortation *Evangelii nuntiandi*, "On Evangelization in the Modern World" (December 8, 1975), popular piety, "if it is well oriented, above all by a pedagogy of evangelization," offers a great good to the life of the Church. Describing the fruits of popular piety, Pope Paul VI observed:

It manifests a thirst for God which only the simple and poor can know. It makes people capable of generosity and sacrifice even to the point of heroism, when it is a question of manifesting belief. It involves an acute awareness of profound attributes of God: fatherhood, providence, loving and constant presence. It engenders interior attitudes rarely observed to the same degree elsewhere: patience, the sense of the Cross in daily life, detachment, openness to others, devotion (*Evangelii nuntiandi*, n. 48d).

The piety and devotion surrounding the Eucharistic miracles down the Christian centuries have borne their richest fruit in the total love of our Lord Jesus Christ in the Blessed Sacrament and in the readiness to give one's life for love of our Eucharistic Lord. The devout study of the Eucharistic miracles inspires in us a deeper awareness and more ardent love of our Lord's Real Presence with us in the Holy Eucharist.

With the publication of *The Eucharistic Miracles of the World*, the remarkable Vatican International Exhibition of the same title can be brought into the homes of the faithful, into parishes and schools, and into the hands of all who desire to come to know or to ponder anew the Mystery of Faith, which is inexhaustible in its richness for our life and salvation. It is my hope that the study of *The Eucharistic Miracles of the World* will inspire in every reader a greater holiness of life, a life patterned on and nourished by the Eucharistic Sacrifice of Christ. In a particular way, it is my hope that it will lead all to a deeper appreciation of the call which our Lord gives to each of us, the call to "put out into the deep," especially by embracing our vocation in life with an undivided heart. For children and young people, may it lead them to reflect upon God's call in their lives and especially to ask God whether He may be calling them to the ordained priesthood or to the consecrated life.

What can bring us greater joy and peace than to draw near to our Lord in the Most Blessed Sacrament? May both the Vatican International Exhibition, *The Eucharistic Miracles of the World*, and the book which memorializes it, be worthy and effective instruments of the New Evangelization. May they lead us to Christ in the Holy Eucharist, so that, one with Christ, we can bring Him to our world.

Adoremus in aeternum Sanctissimum Sacramentum.

The Most Reverend Raymond Leo Burke
Archbishop of Saint Louis
August 6, 2006 — Feast of the Transfiguration of the Lord

PICTURA ALTARIS SS. CORPORIS CHRISTI
OLIM SUPRASCRIPTI MILLESIMO 1547; CUIUS
TITULUS TRANSLATUS FUIT IN HANC
CAPELLAM EX DECRETO EPISCOPALI

Introduction

IN A CATECHESIS ON EUCHARISTIC MIRACLES, WHICH ASPECTS SHOULD BE EMPHASIZED?

I wish, first of all, to highlight certain limits that should be kept in mind in a catechesis on Eucharistic miracles. I will then point out the positive aspects these miracles can offer to such a catechesis.

1) LIMITS:

- **Our faith is not founded on Eucharistic miracles,** but on the proclamation of the Lord Jesus, received with faith through the action of the Holy Spirit. We believe because we have believed in the preaching (see *Gal 3:5*); *"fides ex auditu, auditus autem per verbum Christi"* (*Rom 10:17*): "Faith depends on hearing and hearing by the word of Christ; and, in turn, preaching depends on the word of Christ." "Believing is an act of the intellect, which under the influence of the will moved by God through grace, gives its consent to divine truth" (St. Thomas, *Summa Theologiae*, II-II, q.2, a.9,c).

Our faith in the Eucharist has as its center Christ, Who during His preaching foretold the institution of the Eucharist and then actually instituted It during the celebration of the Last Supper with His Apostles on Holy Thursday.

Since then, the Church, faithful to the command of the Lord, "Do this in memory of me" (*1 Cor 11:24*), has always—with great faith—celebrated the Eucharist, especially on Sunday, the day of Jesus' resurrection, and continues to do so "until He comes" (1 Cor 11:26).

- **A Christian is not obliged to believe in Eucharistic miracles.** These miracles do not bind the faithful to believe in them, even if they are officially recognized by the Church. Every Christian is free to make up his or her own mind. No Christian is obliged to believe in any private revelation, not even those approved by the Church.
- **In principle, however, the believer must not exclude** the possibility that God may intervene in an extraordinary way in any given moment, place, event or person. The difficulty is discerning whether, in an individual case, the authentic extraordinary intervention of God has taken place.
- **The prudence of the Church** in the face of extraordinary phenomena (like Eucharistic miracles), **is fully justified**, since, among other things, one can run into the following risks:
  - thinking that God forgot to tell us something in the institution of the Eucharist;
  - making the Sunday Eucharist a secondary matter;
  - attributing excessive importance to the miraculous and the extraordinary, with the resulting undervaluing of the "everyday dimension" in the life of the believer and of the Church;
  - easily and excessively believing suggestions or illusions.

The Church's approval of a Eucharistic miracle contains the following elements:

- the event in question does not contain anything that contradicts faith and morals;
- it is lawful to make it public;
- the faithful are authorized to give their prudent assent to it.

Even though no one is obliged to believe in them, a believer should show respect for Eucharistic miracles whose authenticity has been recognized by the Church.

2) POSITIVE ASPECTS:

Eucharistic miracles can be useful and fruitful aids to our faith. For example:

- **They help us go beyond the visible and the perceptible** and admit the existence of something *beyond*. Precisely because it is recognized as an extraordinary happening, a Eucharistic miracle has no explanation in scientific facts and reasoning. It goes beyond human reason and challenges a person to "go beyond" the perceptible, the visible, and the human—that is, to admit that there is something incomprehensible, something unexplainable by human reason alone, something that cannot be scientifically demonstrated.

- **They can give rise to an opportunity—especially during catechetical instruction—to speak of *public Revelation* and of its importance to the Church and to Christians.** Eucharistic miracles are all about extraordinary events that have taken place after Jesus' institution of the Eucharist, after the end of the New Testament, that is, after the end of public Revelation.

What is public Revelation?
Public Revelation is something that:
- was progressively disclosed by God, beginning with Abraham, continuing with the prophets, all the way to Jesus Christ;
- is attested to in both parts of the Bible: the Old and the New Testaments;
- is intended for all men and for the entire man, of all times and places;
- is radically different, in essence and not just in degree, from so-called private revelations;
- ended with Christ in the New Testament, to which the Church is bound.

Why did public Revelation end with Christ?

Because Jesus Christ is the mediator and the fullness of Revelation.

"He, being the only-begotten Son of God made man, is the perfect and definitive Word of the Father. In the sending of the Son and the gift of the Spirit, Revelation is now fully complete, although the faith of the Church must gradually grasp its full significance over the course of centuries" (Compendium—Catechism of the Catholic Church, n. 9).

"In times past, God spoke in partial and various ways to our ancestors through the prophets; in these last days, he spoke to us through the Son, whom he made heir of all things and through whom he created the universe" (Heb 1:1-2).

In a word, Christ, Son of God made man, is the unique, perfect and definitive Word of the Father, Who in Him speaks and gives everything, and there will be no other Word than this one.

"Ever since he gave us His Son, Who is the unique and definitive Word, God, in His Word, has told us everything all at one time and has nothing more to tell us" (St. John of the Cross).

"The Christian economy, therefore, since it is the new and definitive covenant, will never pass away; and no new public revelation is to be expected before the glorious manifestation of our Lord, Jesus Christ" (Vatican Council II, Dogmatic Constitution *Dei Verbum*, 4).

What are the consequences of this conclusion regarding public Revelation?

Here are some of them:
- The God of Christians is credible, trustworthy. Revelation is built on the foundation of Holy Scripture and not on messages subsequently handed down to individual believers.

- We cannot expect any manifestation or new revelation from God other than the glorious return of Christ, Who will inaugurate "new heavens and a new earth" (*2 Pet 3:13*), allowing God the Father to be "all in all" (*1 Cor 15-28*).

- The Church is bound to the unique event of sacred history and to the word of the Bible, and her mission is to guarantee, to interpret, to gain a deeper understanding of, and to give witness to public Revelation. This happens thanks to the special assistance of the Holy Spirit, Who is her guide and Who helps her to understand ever better that treasure which is Jesus Christ.

- Public Revelation requires our faith: "In fact, in it, by means of human words and the mediation of the living community of the Church, God himself speaks to us and to every person of whatever race, language, nation, time or place. The certainty that God speaks gives me the assurance that I am encountering truth itself, and thus I have that kind of certainty that cannot be verified in any human form of knowledge. It is the certainty on which I build my life and to which, dying, I entrust myself" (Congregation for the Doctrine of the Faith, *The Message of Fatima*, p. 34).

- Nonetheless, even if Revelation is complete, it is not necessarily fully explicit. It is up to Christian faith to understand it better, deepen its meaning, incarnate it continually, and give witness to it to all people with fidelity and courage. In this way, we can gradually grasp its full significance over the course of the centuries.

- **Eucharistic miracles can help us understand and live the faith, which has Christ and Christ-Eucharist as its center.** These miracles are indeed useful as long as they are closely focused on Christ and do not become autonomous. They can strengthen the subjective faith of believers and even non-believers. Hence they are a help to their faith as long as they lead people to the Eucharist instituted by Christ and celebrated every Sunday. They must serve the faith. They must not and cannot add anything to the one and only definitive gift of Christ-Eucharist, but they can become a humble reminder of it, sometimes leading to a fruitful and deeper knowledge of it. They can become a help that is offered but not one that we are obliged to use.

- Eucharistic miracles can **encourage us to understand, appreciate and love the Eucharist**.

They can help a person rediscover the mystery, the beauty and the richness of the Eucharist. The Compendium of the Catechism of the Catholic Church, approved and published by Pope Benedict XVI, says:

"The Eucharist is the source and summit of all Christian life. In the Eucharist, the sanctifying action of God in our regard and our worship of him reach their high point. It contains the whole spiritual good of the Church, Christ himself, our Pasch. Communion with divine life and the unity of the People of God are both expressed and effected by the Eucharist. Through the Eucharistic celebration we are united already with the liturgy of heaven and we have a foretaste of eternal life" (n. 274).

- We must never forget nor fail to mention that **the Eucharist is the true, great, inexhaustible daily miracle.**

- **It is a sacrament:** "The sacraments, instituted by Christ and entrusted to the Church, are efficacious signs of grace perceptible to the senses. Through them divine life is bestowed upon us. (...) The sacraments are efficacious *ex opere operato* ('by the very fact that the sacramental action is performed'), because it is Christ who acts in the sacraments and communicates the grace they signify. The efficacy of the sacraments does not depend upon the personal holiness of the minister" (Compendium of the Catechism of the Catholic Church, nn. 224 and 229).

- **It is the Sunday sacrament *par excellence.*** We must emphasize the fact that the miracle most common and accessible to all is the one that takes place in our churches whenever Mass is celebrated.

"The Eucharist is the very sacrifice of the Body and Blood of the Lord Jesus which he instituted to perpetuate the sacrifice of the cross throughout the ages until his return in glory. Thus he entrusted to his Church this memorial of his death and Resurrection. It is a sign of unity, a bond of charity, a paschal banquet, in which Christ is consumed, the mind is filled with grace, and a pledge of future glory is given to us" (Compendium, 271).

It is indeed true that the most important and astounding *miracle* is the one that takes place whenever the Eucharist is celebrated, during which **Jesus Christ is present "in a unique and incomparable way."** He is present in a true, real and substantial way, with His Body and Blood, with His Soul and Divinity. "In the Eucharist, therefore, there is present in a sacramental way, that is, under the Eucharistic species of bread and wine, Christ whole and entire, God and Man" (Compendium, n. 282). In making His Sacrifice of the Cross present and actual, He becomes our food and drink, with His Body and His Blood, uniting us with Him and with each other, becoming our viaticum on our earthly pilgrimage toward our eternal homeland.

This is the mysterious miracle *par excellence*, which we are invited to celebrate, especially on Sunday, in the community of the Church, breaking the one bread, which—as St. Ignatius of Antioch affirms—"is the medicine of immortality, the antidote keeping us from death and helping us live in Jesus Christ forever."

- **It would be good to make use of the shrines of the Eucharistic miracles approved by the Church, as places of liturgical celebrations** (especially the celebration of the Sacrament of Reconciliation), as well as other places of prayer and Eucharistic spirituality, of catechesis and the performance of charity.

- **Eucharistic miracles manifest and bring about their relationship with popular piety.**

Often Eucharistic miracles emanate especially from popular piety, and they are reflected in this piety. Miracles give it new energy and reveal new forms to it. This does not prevent them from having an effect on the liturgy itself, as the feast of Corpus Christi shows. The liturgy is the criterion; it is the vital form of the whole Church, which is nourished directly by the Gospel.

d. Raffaello Martinelli

Monsignor Raffaello Martinelli
Rector of the International Ecclesiastical College of St. Charles
Official of the Congregation for the Doctrine of the Faith

The Real Presence

The Eucharist as the Real Presence is the touchstone of sanctity. As evidence of this fact we have the witness of the saints who, when they speak or write about the power of the Blessed Sacrament to sanctify, seem to be positively extreme in their claims about what the Real Presence can achieve in making a sinful person holy.

In order to appreciate the value of the Real Presence in the spiritual life, we must go back in spirit to the event described by St. John when our Lord, after He had worked the miracle of the multiplication of the loaves and fishes, made the solemn promise of the Eucharist.

"I am the Bread of Life," Christ declared on that occasion. "He who comes to me will never be hungry. He who believes in me will never thirst. But, as I have told you, you can see me and still you do not believe. All that the Father gives me will come to me and whoever comes to me, I shall not turn him away because I have come down from heaven, not to do my own will, but to do the will of the one who sent me. Now the will of him who sent me is that I should lose nothing of all that he has given to me and that I should raise it up on the last day. Yes, it is my Father's will that whoever sees the Son and believes in him shall have eternal life and that I shall raise him up on the last day."

By now we have read and heard and meditated on these words many times, but they deserve further reflection because they contain so much mystery that after nineteen centuries of the Church's existence, she has not begun to exhaust the richness of their meaning.

Every time we go back, *every* time we go back to Christ's words of revelation, we always discover something new. Always! The key word in Christ's discourse on the Eucharist is the word *believe*.

On the answer to "What do we believe?" depends in large measure whether we shall only know about sanctity or also attain it, whether holiness will remain only an idea or whether we shall actually become holy. What a difference!

The simplest way to express what Christ asks us to believe about the Real Presence is that the Eucharist is really *He*. The Real Presence is the *real Jesus*. We are to believe that the Eucharist began in the womb of the Virgin Mary; that the flesh which the Son of God received from His Mother at the Incarnation is the same flesh into which He changed bread at the Last Supper; that the blood He received from His Mother is the same blood into which He changed wine at the Last Supper. Had she not given Him His flesh and blood, there could not be a Eucharist.

We are to believe that the Eucharist is Jesus Christ—simply, without qualification. It is God become man in the fullness of His divine nature, in the fullness of

His human nature, in the fullness of His body and soul, in the fullness of everything that makes Jesus Jesus. He is in the Eucharist with His human mind and will united with the Divinity, with His hands and feet, His face and features, with His eyes and lips and ears and nostrils, with His affections and emotions and, with emphasis, with His living, pulsating, physical Sacred Heart. That is what our Catholic Faith demands of us that we believe. If we believe this, we are Catholic. If we do not, we are not, no matter what people may think we are.

Our faith is belief because we do not see what we believe. We accept on Christ's words that all of this is there, or rather, here in the Holy Eucharist. Faith must supply what, as the *Tantum Ergo* sings, "the senses do not perceive." And faith must reveal what the mind by itself cannot see. Let us never forget this phrase, first in Latin, *lumen fidei,* the light of faith. Faith reveals, faith discloses, faith enlightens, faith empowers the mind to see what the mind without faith cannot see.

Strange as it may sound, when we believe in the Real Presence, we believe in things twice unseen. We see only what looks like bread and wine, tastes and smells like bread and wine, and yet we are to believe that behind these physical appearances is a man: faith number one. And we are further to believe that behind the unseen man is God: faith number two.

Is it any wonder the Church calls the Eucharist *Mysterium Fidei, the* Mystery of Faith? Those who accept the Real Presence accept by implication all the cardinal mysteries of Christianity. They believe in the Trinity, in the Father who sent the Son and in the Son who sent the Holy Spirit. They believe in the Incarnation, that the Son of God became man like one of us. They believe in Christ's divinity since no one but God could change bread and wine into His own Body and Blood. They believe in the Holy Catholic Church which Christ founded and in which, through successive generations, is communicated to bishops and priests the incredible power of making Christ continually present among us in the Blessed Sacrament. They believe, against all the betrayals by the Judases of history and all the skepticism of Christ's first disciples, in an unbroken chain of faith ever since Peter replied to Christ's question whether he and his companions also wanted to leave the Master. What a chance Christ took. "Lord," Peter looked around, "to whom shall we go?" (And he spoke for all of us.) "You have the message of eternal life, and we believe, we know, that you are the holy one of God."

There is a prayer in the Coptic Liturgy that I think perfectly answers the first question we are asking. "What do I believe when I believe in the Real Presence?" The prayer goes as follows, a little long, but worth it:

"I believe and I will confess to my last breath that this is the living bread which Your only-begotten Son, our Lord and God and Savior, Jesus Christ, took from our Lady and the Queen of Mankind, the holy, sinless Virgin Mary, Mother of God. He made it one with His Godhead without confusion or change. He witnessed before Pontius Pilate and was of His own free will condemned in our place to the holy tree. Truly I believe that His Godhead was not separated from His manhood for a moment, not even for the twinkle of an eye. He gave His body for the remission of our sins and for eternal life to those who partake of this body. I believe, I believe, I believe that this is in very truth that body. Amen."

That is your faith and mine.

But why do we believe in terms of the promises He made? What blessings and benefits did He assure those who believe in this Eucharistic Mystery? All the blessings that Christ promised to those who believe in the Holy Eucharist are summed up in His own masterful promise of *life*. Those who believe will receive *life* and the life that He promised was *zoé*—the kind of life that belongs to God, the kind of life that Father, Son and Holy Spirit shared and interchanged from all eternity. Those who believe will receive this life. Those who do not believe will die. What kind of life was Christ talking about? It must have been the supernatural life of grace in our souls, of partaking or participation in His own divine life.

This, in homely language, is what the Savior promised those who believed in His Real Presence. He assured them, and therefore assures us, that we shall be not only alive, but filled with His life, full to brimming and flowing over with strength and power and wisdom and peace and all manner of holiness. This is what sanctity is all about. It is the *muchness* of the good things of God. It is the more and more and still more of the life of God in our souls. More still, He promises that, provided that we believe in Him in the Eucharist, He will sustain this life in our souls into eternity. In other words, being alive now, we shall never die. And most marvelous, He will even make this life pour from our souls into our bodies risen from the grave on the last day and glorified by the vision of God.

No wonder the Eucharist is called *panis vitae*, the Bread of Life. It is that, and let us remind ourselves, and here is the condition, one condition, that before we eat this Bread with our lips, we take it by faith into our hearts. Indeed, unless we first have faith, we shall, as Paul tells us, "eat it to our malediction." Only believers can benefit from this Bread of Life, only believers can profit from the Blessed Sacrament, and only believers can grow in spirit by partaking of the Eucharist, depending *always* on the measure of their faith. Those who believe deeply in the Real Presence will benefit greatly from the Real Presence; those who believe weakly will also benefit accordingly. The Eucharist is capable of working miracles in our lives. So it can—after all, the Eucharist is Jesus. He worked—change the tense—He works miracles, but as it depended then (remember, Christ could not work *miracles* in certain places for lack of faith), the same now. It depends on the depth and degree of our faith.

Fr. John A. Hardon, S.J.
Copyright 1998 InterMirifica

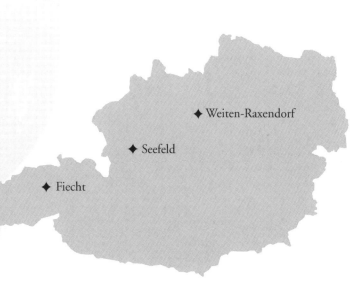

◆ Weiten-Raxendorf

◆ Seefeld

◆ Fiecht

The little village of St. Georgenberg-Fiecht in the Inn Valley is very well-known, especially because of a Eucharistic miracle which took place there in 1310. During Mass, a priest was seized with doubts regarding the Real Presence of Jesus in the consecrated Elements. Right after the Consecration, the wine changed into Blood and began to boil and overflow out of the chalice. In 1480, after 170 years, the Precious Blood was "still fresh as though flowing from a wound," wrote the chronicler of those days. The Precious Blood is preserved intact to this day in a reliquary at the Monastery of St. Georgenberg.

A painting depicting the miracle

*N*ear the side altar of the monastery church there is a tablet which reads: "In the year of grace 1310, under Abbot Rupert, a priest was celebrating Holy Mass in this church dedicated to the holy martyr George and the holy apostle James. After consecrating the wine, he was seized with doubts as to whether the Blood of Christ was really and truly present under the species of wine. Suddenly the wine changed into red Blood that began to boil in the chalice and overflow from it. The abbot and his monks, who happened to be in the choir, and the numerous pilgrims who were present at the celebration, approached the altar and realized what had happened. The priest, terrified, was unable to drink all the Precious Blood, so the abbot placed the remainder in a vessel, alongside the cloth used to wipe the chalice, in the main altar's tabernacle.

"As soon as news of this miraculous event began to spread, more and more pilgrims came to adore the Precious Blood. So great was the number of the Precious Blood's devotees that in 1472 Bishop Georg von Brixen sent the abbot of Wilten, Johannes Lösch, and the pastors, Sigmund Thaur and Kaspar of Absam, to better study the

Silver and gold monstrance from 1719 in which the Precious Blood of the miracle is preserved

The ancient Monastery of St. Georgenberg developed in two complexes, one on the mountain and the other in the valley

phenomenon. As a result of this investigation, adoration of the Precious Blood was encouraged and the miracle was declared authentic.

"Among the devotees were important Church dignitaries, like John, Bishop of Trieste; George, Bishop of Brixen; Rupert, Archbishop of Cologne and Duke of Bavaria; Rupert, Bishop of Chiemsee; Frederick, and many others."

A second documentary tablet recounts how the Relic of the Precious Blood helped preserve the Catholic faith during the Protestant schism: "In 1593, when Luther's teachings were spread-

ing everywhere in Tyrol, the monks of St. Georgenberg were asked to preach the faith everywhere. Abbot Michael Geisser was preaching with great success before a large crowd in the parish church of Schwaz and did not hesitate to recall the Holy Miracle of the Blood as proof of the Real Presence of Jesus Christ in the Blessed Sacrament of the Altar. He disputed in such a convincing way that his adversaries were obliged to leave the scene. This total victory over false teaching was regarded by believers as a special grace the Lord was granting His faithful, the adorers of the Precious Blood."

The little town of Seefeld is the goal of many pilgrimages because of the Eucharistic miracle which took place there in 1384. During one Holy Thursday Mass, a nobleman by the name of Oswald Milser expected the priest to give him the large Host for Communion. Just as he was about to receive Communion, the pavement began to tremble beneath him, and Oswald felt as if he were being sucked into it. As the priest was returning the Host to the altar, living Blood began to flow from the Sacred Species.

Miracle of Seefeld. Detail of the ceiling

In the little town of Seefeld, Oswald Milser, Lord of Schlossberg, arrogantly expected, at one Holy Thursday Mass, to receive a large Host like that of the celebrating priest. But at the moment he was about to receive Communion, the pavement began to tremble and broke open. Oswald grasped the altar so as not to fall, and the priest immediately retrieved the Host from the man's mouth. The trembling stopped, and living Blood began to flow from the Host. There were many witnesses of the miracle, and very soon the news spread throughout the whole nation. The Emperor Maximilian I himself was very devoted to the miracle. Today one can visit the Church of St. Oswald where the precious relic of the Host, stained with Blood, is exposed, and can also view many paintings depicting the miracle.

Painting of the Miracle of Seefeld, preserved in the Elsbethenkapelle ad Hopfgarten

An old painting of the miracle

Altar of the miracle

Frescoes in the church depicting the miracle

Church of St. Oswald

Elsbethenkapelle ad Hopfgarten in the Brixen area of Tyrol, built in 1494 by the pastor, Bartholomäus Hamersbach

Representation of the Miracle of Seefeld. Detail of the Gothic gable, Church of St. Oswald (1470)

Main altar of the Church of St. Oswald, Seefeld

Banner in the Church of St. Oswald depicting the miracle

In fifteenth-century Austria there were a number of thefts of consecrated Hosts, so Church authorities began keeping the Hosts in the sacristy. Despite these precautions, in 1411 a thief succeeded in stealing a consecrated Host from the parish church in Weiten. The Host fell unnoticed to the ground during his escape and was discovered several days later by a pious woman. The Host was radiant, and was divided into two pieces which were joined by threads of bleeding Flesh.

Weiten's parish church

According to records from the village of Weiten, the theft occurred in 1411. In the parish church, a thief broke into the sacristy and stole a consecrated Host, slipping It into one of his gloves. He then mounted his horse, intending to make for the nearby village of Spitz. Instead of taking the main road, he chose a side road passing through the valley of Mühldorf and known as "Am Schuß." When he arrived at a certain spot (which today is marked by a chapel in honor of the miracle), his horse halted and would not move, no matter how much the man beat him. Some laborers working in the surrounding fields came to help. But there was no way to make the horse move; it stood still as a statue. Then, without warning, the animal leaped to a gallop, and the Host hidden in the rider's glove dropped to the ground without anyone's noticing.

A few days later, a Mrs. Scheck from Mannersdorf passed by the spot and saw the Host near a hedge, encircled by a bright light. In great wonder, she picked up the Holy Eucharist and noticed that the consecrated Host was broken into two parts joined together by threads of bleeding Flesh. Greatly moved, in thanksgiving, she built a

Panoramic view of Weiten

Painting in the parish of Weiten depicting the miracle

Chapel built on the exact spot where the Host was found

small chapel on the spot at her own expense. As news of the miracle spread, many pilgrims came to the place. Later, it became necessary to build a larger church to contain the great crowds that came on pilgrimage each year to honor the precious relic.

Eucharistic Miracles of
BELGIUM

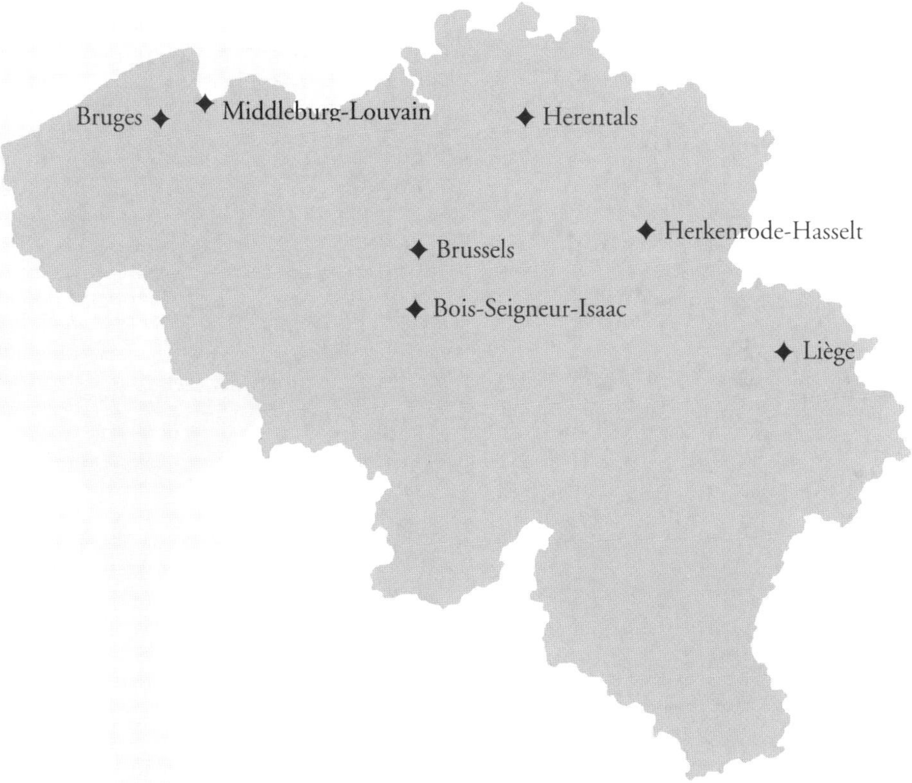
Bruges
Middleburg-Louvain
Herentals
Herkenrode-Hasselt
Brussels
Bois-Seigneur-Isaac
Liège

In the Eucharistic miracle of Bois-Seigneur-Isaac, the consecrated Host bled and stained the corporal during Mass. On May 3, 1413, the Bishop of Cambrai, Peter d'Ailly, authorized devotion to the sacred relic. The first procession took place in 1414. On January 13th, 1424, Pope Martin V officially approved the building of the Monastery of Bois-Seigneur-Isaac. Even today the monastery is the goal of pilgrimages, and the sacred relic of the corporal stained with Blood can still be venerated in the chapel.

Choir of the Chapel of the Precious Blood

*B*eginning on the Tuesday before Pentecost of the year 1405, the Lord appeared, covered with wounds, to John of Huldenberg, the owner of the place. Only during the third apparition did Our Lord speak, ordering John, *"Go to the Chapel of Isaac; you will find Me there."* At the same time, the parish priest, Peter Ost, heard a voice instructing him to offer the Mass of the Holy Cross in the Chapel of Isaac. The following day the pastor summoned all the faithful to assist at Mass in that chapel.

John of Huldenberg was among those present. The priest began the Mass, and when he unfolded the corporal, he saw there a Particle of the large Host which had been consecrated the preceding Tuesday. He sought to consume the Host, but the Eucharist clung to the corporal and began to bleed. The priest turned white, and John, who had observed everything, comforted him by saying: "Do not fear, this marvel comes from God," and related his visions.

For four days, that is, until the Tuesday after Pentecost, the Blood continued to flow, leaving a stain the length of a finger by three fingers wide. Then,

Main altar, Laurent Delvaux (18th century)

Reliquary of the True Cross

Relic of a thorn from Jesus' crown

Painting of the Castle and Abbey of Bois-Seigneur-Isaac

Relic of the Eucharistic miracle, corporal stained with Blood

Sanctuary of the Precious Blood, Relics Chapel

Picture of the altar where the curé of Haut-Ittre celebrated the Holy Mass during which the miracle took place

Premonstratensian Abbey, Chapel of the Precious Blood

Interior of the Chapel of the Precious Blood

having stained almost the entire corporal, the Blood coagulated little by little and dried up. The miracle was seen and attested to by many. The Bishop of Cambrai, Peter d' Ailly, informed of what happened, wished to personally investigate and had the corporal in his care for some two years. Every attempt to remove the stain of Blood from the corporal was useless.

The Bishop opened an investigation in which testimonies were gathered regarding the prodigies wrought by the relic of the Precious Blood. On June 16, 1410, the Bishop granted an indulgence of 40 days to those who visited the chapel at Bois-Seigneur-Isaac. On May 3, 1413, he allowed the corporal to be venerated as a relic and established a solemn procession in honor of the miracle, along with public exposition of the Blessed Sacrament. Even today, every year on the Sunday following the feast of the Birth of Mary, the citizens of Bois-Seigneur-Isaac come together in prayer to celebrate the memory of this Eucharistic miracle.

The oldest documents concerning the Precious Blood of Bruges date back to 1256. The Precious Blood was probably part of a group of relics of the Passion of Christ preserved at the Imperial Museum of Bucoleon in Constantinople (modern Istanbul). In 1203 Constantinople was besieged and conquered by the Crusaders. Baldwin IX, Count of Flanders, after being crowned as the new emperor, sent the relic of the Precious Blood to Bruges in his native country.

Interior of the Church of the Most Precious Blood, Bruges

Recent analyses were made of the crystal bottle containing the Precious Blood. The bottle has been dated back to the 11th century, and it was made in an area near Constantinople. Although in the Bible there is no explicit mention that the Blood of Christ was ever preserved, in one of the Apocryphal Gospels it is narrated that Joseph of Arimathea preserved some drops of the Blood of Christ.

According to an ancient tradition, Count Diederik van den Elzas brought the bottle containing the Blood of Christ from Jerusalem to Bruges dur-

ing the Second Crusade. Recent investigations, however, have indicated that the relic arrived in Bruges at a later date, probably around 1250, and came from Constantinople.

The adoration of the relic gave rise to the famous international procession that is held each year through the streets of the city on the Feast of the Ascension. The citizens of Bruges dress in historical costumes and reenact biblical scenes and the arrival of the Count of Flanders who brought the sacred relic.

An actor playing the
part of the Count of
Flanders bringing back
the Most Precious Blood

Procession in honor of the
Most Precious Blood

Relic of the Most Precious Blood

A scene in Bruges

Church of the Most Precious Blood

In the cathedral in Brussels there are many artistic testimonies to a Eucharistic miracle which took place in 1370. Desecrators stole some consecrated Hosts and pierced Them with knives as an act of rebellion. From these Hosts came a flow of living Blood. This miracle was venerated up until just a few decades ago. There are many reliquaries of different eras which have been used to contain the miraculous Hosts of the *Miracle du Saint Sacrement*. These reliquaries have been kept to this day in the museum near the cathedral, in an ancient chapel of the Blessed Sacrament. There are also 18th-century tapestries representing the miraculous event.

The five stained-glass windows gracing the side nave of the cathedral take us through the stages of this Eucharistic miracle. They were installed at various times from 1436 to 1870. The kings of Belgium, Leopold I and Leopold II, presented the first windows on the lower level. The others were gifts from various noble families of the country.

The first ten windows (eight on the right side of the nave, close to the choir loft, and two below on the left side of the nave) represent the history of the miracle as it came to Brussels in the middle of the 15th century. The ancient document reads: "In 1369 a rich merchant from Enghien who hated the Catholic religion, had some consecrated Hosts stolen. He worked with a young man from Louvain (windows 1-3). The merchant was assassinated mysteriously a few days later. His widow, surmising that this was a punishment from Heaven, immediately got rid of the Hosts by giving them to friends of her husband. These friends were also enemies of religion.

"On Good Friday 1370, the friends met in a private ceremony and began

Old prints portraying the miracle

Stained glass windows of the cathedral depicting events connected with the Eucharistic miracle

Interior of the Cathedral of St. Gudala and St. Michael, Brussels

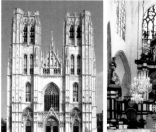

Cathedral of St. Gudala and St. Michael, Brussels

to slash the Hosts with knives (windows 1-5), and the Hosts began to bleed! (windows 4-5). The desecrators were badly frightened and in their turn entrusted the Hosts to a well-known Catholic merchant.

"This merchant revealed the whole story to the curate of the Church of Notre Dame de la Chappelle in Brussels. The curate took possession of the Hosts (windows 6-7) and the desecrators were condemned to death by the Duke of Brabant (windows 8-9). The Hosts were taken in procession to the Cathedral of St. Gudula" (window

The Eucharistic Miracle of Brussels. Hiéron Museum, Paray-le-Monial

Section of a stained glass window in the Cathedral of St. Gudala and St. Michael, in which the Eucharistic miracle is depicted

10). The Eucharistic miracle remains an important part of the traditions of Brussels and is something of a national symbol.

In the Eucharistic miracle of Herentals, some stolen Hosts were found after eight days, perfectly intact in spite of the rain. The Hosts were found in a field near a rabbit burrow, surrounded by a bright light and arranged in the form of a cross. Every year, two paintings by Antoon van Ysendyck depicting the miracle are taken in procession to the field, where a small shrine, *De Hegge,* was built. Here a commemorative Mass is celebrated before numerous faithful. The two paintings are presently kept in the Cathedral of Sint-Waldetrudiskerk, Herentals.

*I*n 1412, a certain Jan van Langerstede found lodging in a hotel not far from the little town of Herentals. This man made a living by stealing sacred objects from churches and selling them all over Europe.

The day after his arrival in Herentals, he went to the nearby village of Poederle, entered the parish church, and, without being seen, stole the chalice and the ciborium containing five consecrated Hosts. As he was returning to Herentals in the place known as *De Hegge* ("the hedge"), he was held back by a mysterious force which prevented

him from continuing his journey. So he tried to rid himself of the Hosts by throwing Them into the river, but his every attempt to do so was useless. Jan was on the verge of despair when he saw a nearby field with a big rabbit burrow where he immediately hid the Hosts. He accomplished this without any trouble and calmly returned to Herentals. In the meantime, the city judge, Gilbert De Pape, began an investigation to find out who had committed the theft in Poederle's church. Among the suspects was Jan. The police searched his luggage and found the chalice and the ciborium.

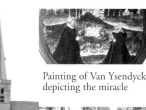

Painting of Van Ysendyck depicting the miracle

Church of St. Waldetrudis, Herentals

Interior of the Church of St. Waldetrudis

The "De Hegge" chapel built at the place where the miracle took place

A. Van Ysendyck (1801-1875). A series of paintings *Het wonder van de Hegge* - The Holy Miracle of the Fence, Church of St. Waldetrudis

Jan then confessed everything except the fact that he had thrown the Hosts away. He was to be immediately hanged and had already climbed the scaffold, when, encouraged by the priest to cleanse his soul before dying, he completely confessed his guilt. The judge then suspended the execution and ordered Jan to indicate the exact place where he had left the stolen Hosts. A large crowd followed them. As soon as they arrived in the field, they saw the Hosts all radiant, arranged in the form of a cross. Strangely, the Hosts were intact, notwithstanding the weather, and they were at once brought back in procession, some to Herentals and some to Poederle, where they remained until the 16th century.

On January 2, 1441, the miracle was declared authentic by the magistrate of Herentals. At the place where the Hosts were found, a small chapel was built which was visited by numerous prelates, such as Jean Malderus, Bishop of Anvers, in 1620, and Pope Benedict XIV in 1749. The daughter of John of Luxembourg, Elizabeth Van Görlitz, paid for the expansion of the chapel, which was later transformed into a shrine.

In the Cathedral of St. Quintinus in Hasselt is exposed the relic of a Eucharistic miracle which took place in Herkenrode in 1317. During the course of the centuries, many tests have been carried out to verify the miraculous preservation of the consecrated Host from which Blood flowed. We recall the test done in the 18th century by the Apostolic Nuncio Carafa and the Bishop of Liège, and the one done by the Archbishop of Malines during a visit of the Archduchess Isabel. In the cathedral we also find numerous paintings depicting the miracle, done by a pupil of Jordaens, Jan van Boeckhorst.

Monstrance used to carry the relic of the miraculous Host in procession

On July 25, 1317, the pastor of the church in Viversel was called to the bedside of one his parishioners who was seriously ill and wanted to receive the sacraments. Upon his arrival at the sick person's house, the priest set his bag containing the consecrated Host on a table near the door and went to hear the sick person's confession. One of the family members, curious about the bag, opened it on the sly. From it he pulled out the pyx, opened the cover and put his hand into it. As soon as he realized there was a Host inside, he immediately put everything back. In the meantime, the priest came out from the sick person's room to get the Host in order to give him Communion. When he opened the bag with the pyx inside, he saw that the Host he himself had consecrated during Mass was stained with Blood and was stuck to the linen covering the bottom of the container. Troubled and panic-stricken, he made up an excuse and rushed out of the house. He went to the pastor of nearby Lumen to tell him what had happened. The latter advised him to bring the Host to the Abbey of Herkenrode. It was August 1, 1317.

The priest left, taking the pyx with him. Along the road, extraordinary things happened. As soon as he arrived at the Benedictine monastery, he showed the Host stained with Blood to all the religious. Then, the face of Christ crowned with thorns appeared on the Host. This was attested to by numerous witnesses.

Church of St. Quintinus in Hasselt

In 1854, the Palmers family built this small chapel in the place called Sacramentsberg in memory of the Eucharistic miracle

Old prints depicting the miracle

Interior of Church of St. Quintinus, Hasselt

The main altar in the Church of St. Quintinus, Hasselt

An old document describing the miracle

Procession in honor of the miracle

Relic of the miraculous Host

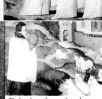

Painting kept in the Cathedral of Hasselt where the flock can be seen respectfully kneeling at the passing of the priest carrying the sacred relic in the place called Sacramentsberg

In the cathedral in Hasselt there is a painting depicting a flock of sheep kneeling as the priest, carrying the Eucharist, passes by. In this place, called *Sacramentsberg,* a chapel was built as a perpetual memorial. From that time on, "the Blessed Sacrament of the Miracle," which had been placed in a reliquary and exposed for public veneration, worked various cures and more than once protected the monastery of Herkenrode from fire. The relic of the miracle was kept at the Abbey from 1796 until 1804, when It was transferred to the Cathedral of St. Quintinus in Hasselt.

Paintings by Jan van Boeckhorst depicting the scenes of the miracle, Cathedral of Hasselt

The altar where part of the relic of the miraculous Host is kept

Closeup of the miraculous Host

This Eucharistic miracle dates back to 1374. In St. Peter's Church in Middleburg, during Holy Communion, the consecrated Host changed into bleeding Flesh. A portion of the Host is kept to this day in Louvain by the Augustinian Fathers. The monk Jean de Gheest, confessor to the Archbishop who approved the cult, asked for the precious relic as a gift. The other portion is in St. Peter's Church in Middleburg.

Painting depicting the miracle, St. James Church, Louvain

*T*here is abundant documentation available on this Eucharistic miracle. In a monograph written in 1905 by historian Jos Wils, professor at the Catholic University of Louvain, entitled *Le Sacrement du Miracle de Louvain,* are cited almost all the contemporary documents and testimonies. In Middleburg lived a noble woman known by all for her great faith and devotion. The woman was also very attentive to the spiritual formation of her family and household staff. During Lent of 1374, as every year, all in the household began to do penance in preparation for Easter. A few days

before that, a new manservant by the name of John had been hired. He had not gone to confession in many years, despite the dissolute life he was living. The woman invited all the household staff to go to Mass. John did not dare oppose this invitation so as not to disappoint her. He attended the whole Eucharistic celebration, and when it was time to receive Holy Communion, the man approached the altar with much superficiality.

As soon as he received the Host on his tongue, It changed into bleeding Flesh. At once John took the Host from his

Altar where the miracle took place

St. James Church in Louvain

mouth; Blood dripped from the Sacred Flesh onto the cloth covering the altar rail. The priest realized at once what was happening, and with great emotion, carefully placed the miraculous Host in a vessel inside the tabernacle. John repented and confessed his sin before everyone. From that day on, he led an exemplary life and demonstrated great devotion to the Most Blessed Sacrament to the end of his life. All the Church and civil authorities of the city were informed of what had happened, and after diligent investigation, the Archbishop authorized the cult of this miraculous event.

◆ Tumaco

The 1906 tsunami on the Pacific Coast caused enormous destruction in many areas. Fr. Bernardino Garcia de la Concepción, who at the time was in Panama City, gave the following testimony regarding the terrible cataclysm. "Suddenly an enormous wave crashed into the port, reaching into the market area and washing everything away. Boats which had been drawn up on shore were picked up and hurled long distances, causing heavy losses." The tiny island of Tumaco was spared by a miracle, thanks to the faith of the people in the Most Blessed Sacrament.

On January 31, 1906, on the tiny island of Tumaco, at 10 o'clock in the morning, the earth shook violently for about ten minutes. All the inhabitants of the village ran to the church and begged the pastor, Fr. Gerard Larrondo, and Fr. Julián to lead a procession with the Blessed Sacrament. The sea was rising and had already engulfed part of the beach. A huge wall of water was building up into one gigantic wave.

Frightened, Fr. Gerard consumed the small Hosts in the ciborium and set the large Host aside. Turning to the people, he called out: "Let us go, my children. Let us all go toward the beach, and may God have mercy on us." Comforted by the presence of Jesus in the Eucharist, they began their march, weeping and crying out to God.

Scarcely had Fr. Larrondo reached the beach with monstrance in hand when he advanced courageously to the water's edge, and just as the wave came rushing in, he calmly raised the Sacred Host, his heart filled with faith, and traced the sign of the Cross in the air. It was a moment of tremendous solemnity. The wave came a little closer, but

Beach at Tumaco (Columbia)

Tumaco at the time of the 1906 miracle

before Fr. Larrondo and Fr. Julián, who was beside him, realized what was happening, the people, amazed and moved, shouted, "Miracle, miracle!" In truth, an invisible force beyond that of nature prevailed. The mighty wall of water which had threatened to wipe the village of Tumaco off the face of the earth had suddenly halted and begun to recede, and the sea quickly returned to its normal level. The inhabitants of Tumaco were overcome with joy at having been saved from death by Jesus in the Blessed Sacrament. Prayers of fervent thanks arose on all sides.

News of the miracle of Tumaco spread throughout the world, and Fr. Larrondo received numerous letters from Europe asking for his prayers.

♦ Ludbreg

During a Mass in Ludbreg in 1411, a priest doubted whether the Body and Blood of Christ were really present in the Eucharistic species. Immediately after being consecrated, the wine turned into Blood. Today the precious relic of the miraculous Blood still draws thousands of the faithful, and every year, in early September, the so-called *Sveta Nedilja* or "Holy Sunday" is celebrated for an entire week in honor of the Eucharistic miracle of 1411.

Fresco depicting the miracle

*I*n 1411 at Ludbreg, in the chapel of Count Batthyany's castle, a priest was celebrating Mass. During the consecration of the wine, the priest doubted the truth of transubstantiation. Just then the wine in the chalice turned into Blood. Not knowing what to do, the priest sealed up the relic in the wall behind the main altar. The workman who did the job was sworn to silence.

The priest also kept it a secret and revealed it only on his deathbed. After the priest's revelation, news spread quickly and people started coming on pilgrimage to Ludbreg. The Holy See later had the relic of the miracle brought to Rome, where it remained for several years. The people of Ludbreg and the surrounding area, however, continued to make pilgrimages to the castle chapel. In the early 1500s, during the pontificate of Pope Julius II, a commission was convened in Ludbreg to investigate the facts connected with the Eucharistic miracle. Many people testified that they had received marvelous cures while praying in the relic's presence. On April 14, 1513, Pope Leo X published a bull permitting veneration of the holy relic which he himself

In 1753, the Batthyany family had Mihael Peck decorate the castle chapel where the miracle took place with frescoes depicting the events of the miracle

Fresco depicting the procession held in Rome in 1513, in which Pope Leo X carried the precious relic through the city streets

Since 1721, the relic of the Precious Blood has been kept in a precious monstrance by the Augsburg goldsmiths' school, commissioned by Countess Eleonora Batthyany-Strattman, who gave it as a gift to the church in Ludbreg

Interior of the chapel of the Batthyany family castle

had carried in procession several times through the streets of Rome. The relic was later returned to Croatia.

In the 18th century, the northern part of Croatia was ravaged by the plague. The people turned to God for help, and the Croatian parliament did the same. During the session held on December 15, 1739, in the city of Varazdin, they vowed to build a chapel at Ludbreg in honor of the miracle if the plague ended. The plague was averted, but the promised vow was only fulfilled in 1994, when democracy was restored in Croatia.

In 2005, in the votive chapel, the artist Marijan Jakubin painted a large fresco of the Last Supper in which Croatian saints and blesseds were drawn in place of the Apostles. St. John was replaced with Blessed Ivan Merz, who was included among the 18 most important Eucharistic saints in the Church's history during the Synod of Bishops held in Rome in 2005. In the painting, Christ is holding in His hand a monstrance containing the relic of the Eucharistic miracle.

The relic of Blood is still perfectly preserved and is kept in a precious monstrance commissioned by Countess Eleonora Batthyany-Strattman in 1721.

Marijan Jakubin, *The Last Supper*, Shrine of the Miracle of the Precious Blood, Ludbreg

Shrine of the Miracle of the Precious Blood, Ludbreg

Interior of the shrine

Procession held every year in September, during the week when the miracle called *Sveta Nedilja* is celebrated

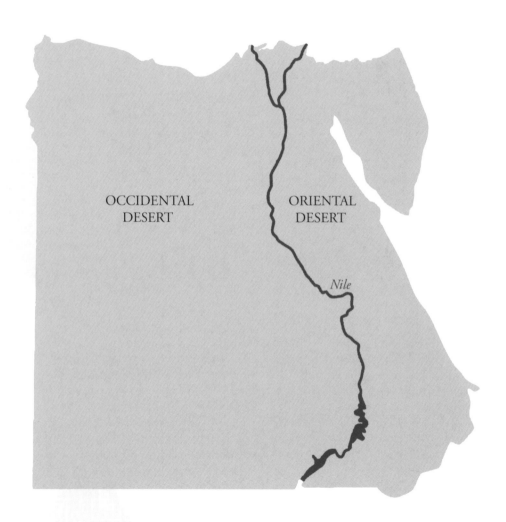

OCCIDENTAL
DESERT

ORIENTAL
DESERT

Nile

The account of this Eucharistic miracle goes back to the first centuries of Christianity and is found in the collection of apothegms of the Fathers of the Desert who lived as hermits in Egypt following the example of St. Anthony the Abbot. A monk was assailed by strong doubts regarding the Real Presence of Jesus in the bread and wine consecrated at Mass. After the Consecration the Infant Jesus was seen in place of the bread. Three other monks who were assisting at the Mass witnessed the same vision.

*I*n the sayings and deeds of the Desert Fathers, we find a description of an ancient Eucharistic miracle. Fr. Daniel the Faranite attests: "Our Fr. Arsenius told us of a monk of Skete who was a hard worker but lacked instruction in the Faith. In his ignorance he would say: 'The Bread we receive is not really the Body of Christ, but a symbol of that Body.' Two of the more experienced monks heard his statement and, knowing that he was a good and pious monk, decided to speak to him since they attributed his words to ignorance rather than to malice. So they went to him and said: 'Father, we heard someone saying something contrary to the Faith: that the bread we receive is not really the Body of Christ, but a symbol.' The priest said, 'I am the one who says this!' They then

began to exhort him, 'You must not believe that, but rather believe what the Catholic Church teaches. We believe that this bread is the Body of Christ, and this chalice is the Blood of Christ, really and truly, and not a symbol.' The accused replied: 'Unless you can show me evidence, I will not change my mind.' The other monks told him: 'This week we will pray to God about this mystery, and we believe that God will show us the truth.'

"At the end of the week, on Sunday, all three went to the church and stood together. The priest was between the two monks on a step. Their eyes were opened: when the Bread was placed on the altar in sacrifice, in place of the Host, the three of them, and only they, saw a Child. When the priest

Ancient Coptic monastery dedicated to St. Paul on the coast of the Red Sea

Monastery of St. Anthony the Abbot in Egypt

Christ embracing Abbot Mena (6th century)

St. Moses, desert monk

Christ enthroned and the Virgin surrounded by saints in the Monastery of Apollo at Bawit

Detail of the painting of Bl. Fra Angelico: *St. Anthony the Abbot in the Desert*

Monastery of St. Paul

Section of the Monastery of St. Anthony the Abbot at the foot of Mt. Qulzum

reached towards the Bread to pick It up and break It, an angel appeared with a sword and pierced the Boy, Whose Blood ran into the chalice. When the priest broke the Bread into pieces, the angel cut little pieces from the Child. When the three monks came up for Communion, the priest was offered bleeding Flesh. At this the doubter was overcome with fear and cried out, 'Lord, I believe that the Bread is Your Body, and that Your Blood is in the chalice!' Immediately the bloodied Flesh he had in his hand took on the appearances of bread, and he communicated, giving thanks to God."

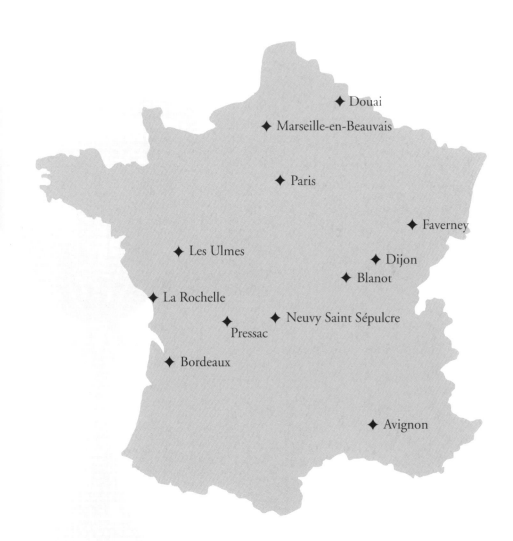

◆ Douai

◆ Marseille-en-Beauvais

◆ Paris

◆ Faverney

◆ Les Ulmes

◆ Dijon

◆ Blanot

◆ La Rochelle

◆ Neuvy Saint Sépulcre

◆ Pressac

◆ Bordeaux

◆ Avignon

On November 30, 1433, the Blessed Sacrament was exposed for public adoration in a small chapel cared for by a confraternity known as "the Gray Penitents." Suddenly, Avignon was flooded when the Rodano, the river crossing the city, overflowed. By boat, two members of the confraternity managed to reach the chapel where the Blessed Sacrament had been left for adoration and was now unattended. When they entered the chapel, they saw that the waters were divided to the right and to the left, leaving the altar and the monstrance perfectly dry.

Old engraving of the Miracle of Avignon

*T*he Eucharistic miracle of Avignon occurred in the Chapel of the Holy Cross, home of the Gray Penitents, whose founding goes back to the time of pious King Louis VIII. This king, in order to celebrate his victory over the Albigensian heretics who denied the Real Presence of Jesus in the Eucharist, had organized a solemn act of reparation on September 14, 1226, the liturgical feast of the Exaltation of the Cross.

In the official documentation of this event, which is still preserved in the chapel of the Gray Penitents, we read that on November 30, 1433, while the Blessed Sacrament was exposed in the little chapel for public adoration, the city of Avignon was hit by a terrible flood. The Rodano River overflowed after days of heavy rain. In the confusion, Armand and Jehan de Pouzilhac-Farure, the latter being the head of the confraternity at the time, with great effort struggled to reach the chapel by boat in order to save the monstrance containing the Blessed Sacrament.

From the gates the two men looked into the chapel toward the altar to see what had happened to the monstrance.

The altar where the miracle took place

Stained-glass window inside the church, depicting the miracle

A carved stone describing the miracle

Stained-glass window in the chapel

They saw that the water, which was almost six feet deep inside the chapel, had parted to the right and to the left of the altar, like two walls, and the altar and the monstrance had remained dry and untouched.

News of the miracle spread rapidly, and all the people, together with the authorities, hastened to the place singing hymns of praise and thanksgiving to the Lord. Several hundred persons witnessed the miracle. The Confraternity of the Gray Penitents decided that the anniversary of the miracle would be celebrated each year in the chapel on the feast of St. Andrew the Apostle.

Even today, every November 30th, the brothers gather at the *Chapelle des Pénitents Gris* to celebrate the memory of the miracle. Before Benediction, the brothers sing a sacred chant taken from the Canticle of Moses, which was composed after the parting of the Red Sea: *"I will sing to the LORD, for he is gloriously triumphant ... At a breath of your anger the waters piled up, the flowing waters stood like a mound, the flood waters congealed in the midst of the sea ... In your mercy you led the people you redeemed; in your strength you guided them to your holy dwelling"* (Exodus 15:1-18).

The news spread rapidly, and many people, including those in authority, came to the chapel, singing songs of praise and thanks to the Lord.

Habit of the Gray Penitents

Gabriel de Vidaud Latour, the first leader of the Gray Penitents

Canal near the chapel

Palace of the Popes, Avignon

Facade of the Chapel of the Gray Penitents

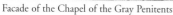

Fresco in the chapel

The Eucharistic miracle of Blanot took place during Easter Mass of 1331. During Communion, the priest accidentally dropped a Host onto the cloth held below the communicant's mouth. The priest tried to pick up the Holy Eucharist, but was unable to do so. The Host had changed into Blood, resulting in a large stain on the cloth. The cloth is still preserved today in the village of Blanot.

Monstrance containing the relic of the miracle

*I*n the 14th century, Blanot was a small village in the center of France and fell within the diocese of Autun. The Bishop of the town, Pierre Bertrand, asked one of his curia officials, Jean Jarossier, to carry out the official investigation the same year that the miracle occurred. The official's document gives us a detailed description of what happened.

"On Easter Sunday, 1331, the first Mass of the day was offered by Hugues de la Baume, the vicar of Blanot. As the priest was giving Holy Communion to Jacquette, the widow of Regnaut d'Effour, a Fragment of the consecrated Host fell onto the cloth held by two men, one of whom was Thomas Caillot. Jacquette did not notice anything, but Thomas, who was holding the cloth, saw it happen and told the priest, who was already placing the ciborium on the altar. 'Father, come quickly, the Body of Our Lord fell from this woman's mouth onto the cloth.' The celebrant immediately returned to pick up the Particle, but suddenly the Fragment, which was about the size of a fifth of a Host, disappeared, and in Its place appeared a drop of Blood. Seeing this, the vicar immediately carried the cloth into the sacristy and began to wash the stained part with water. He washed and scrubbed it repeatedly, but the stain only became redder and larger.

"The vicar, amazed and moved to tears, asked Thomas Caillot for a knife and immediately cut out the stained part of the cloth right on the altar, plac-

A 17th-century display case containing the cloth stained with blood, preserved in a crystal tube at Blanot

LE JOUR DE PÂQUES MCCCXXXI
HUGUES DE BAUME VICAIRE DE BLANOT
CÉLÉBRANT LA MESSE
UNE PARCELLE D'HOSTIE TOMBA
ET SE TRANSFORMA EN GOUTTE DE SANG
SUR LA NAPPE DE COMMUNION.
L'OFFICIAL DE PIERRE BERTRAND
EVÊQUE D'AUTUN
FIT L'ENQUÊTE CANONIQUE.
LE PAPE JEAN XXII
ACCORDA DES INDULGENCES.

Ancient memorial describing the miracle

View of the village of Blanot

Details of paintings decorating the monstrance

Parish of Blanot

ing it in a reliquary after showing it to the people. Then, trembling with emotion, he exclaimed, 'Good people, this is the Precious Blood of Our Lord Jesus Christ, because I tried in every way possible to wash It out, but I can't remove It from this cloth.'"

Every year particular honor is given to the relic of the miracle in Blanot on the feast of Corpus Christi. The Hosts remaining in the ciborium after the distribution of Holy Communion that Easter Sunday were also returned to the tabernacle, never to be distributed. Hundreds of years later they were found to be perfectly preserved.

Procession in honor of the miracle

BORDEAUX

In the Eucharistic miracle of Bordeaux, for more than twenty minutes, Jesus appeared in the Host exposed for public adoration, giving a blessing. Even today it is possible to visit the chapel of the miracle and venerate the precious relic of the monstrance of the apparition, which is kept in Martillac, France, in the church belonging to the contemplative community "La Solitude."

Mother Rita Bonnat, first mother general of the community, with two little orphans

The Eucharistic miracle of Bordeaux is closely connected with the community founded in 1820 by the Venerable Father Pierre Noaille. The community is still active today, especially in Asia and Africa. The marvel occurred twenty months after the foundation of the community in their Church of St. Eulalia on Rue Mazarin, Bordeaux. Jesus appeared in the Host immediately after Abbot Delort, who was substituting for Fr. Noaille that day at the liturgical celebrations, presided over Benediction with the Blessed Sacrament.

For more than twenty minutes, the numerous faithful present were able to contemplate the apparition of Jesus giving a blessing, which was visible on the Host exposed for public adoration. In addition, someone testified that he heard Jesus saying: "I Am He Who Is." This event was approved by the ecclesiastical authorities, among whom was the Archbishop of Bordeaux, Monsignor D'Aviau, who personally heard the testimonies of the faithful who saw the marvel. Even today it is possible to visit the chapel of the miracle and venerate the precious monstrance of the apparition.

La Solitude, Martillac (France), Monastery of the Holy Family

Monstrance containing the miracle

Pierre-Bienvenu Noaille, founder of the religious community of the Holy Family – Our Lady of Loretto

Interior of the church at La Solitude

Church of St. Eulalia in Bordeaux

The Eucharistic Miracle of
DIJON
FRANCE, 1430

In the Eucharistic miracle of Dijon, a woman purchased a stolen monstrance which contained a large Host. The lady used a knife to remove the Host, from which living Blood began to flow. The Blood dried immediately, leaving imprinted on the Host an image of the Lord seated on a semicircular throne with some of the instruments of the Passion at His side. The Host remained intact for more than 350 years until It was destroyed by the revolutionaries in 1794.

Basilica of St. Michael, Dijon

In 1430, in Monaco, a woman purchased a monstrance from a second-hand dealer. The monstrance was most likely stolen because it still contained a large Host used for adoration. The lady, being very ignorant in regard to the Real Presence of Christ in the Eucharist, decided to remove the Host from the monstrance with a knife. Unexpectedly, living Blood began to flow from the Host. The Blood dried immediately, leaving imprinted on the Host an image of the Lord, seated on a semicircular throne with some of the instruments of the Passion at His side.

The lady, horrified, went to Canon Anelon, who took the Host and kept It. The episode quickly came to be known even by the Pope, Eugene IV, who gave the miraculous Host to Duke Phillip of Burgundy, who in turn gave It to the city of Dijon. We know with certainty that in 1794 the miraculous Host was still in the Basilica of Saint Michael the Archangel, but on February 9 of that year, the municipality of Dijon requisitioned the church to consecrate it as a temple of the new sect of "la Raison," that is, of the "goddess of reason." The miraculous Host was burned.

Many are the documents and works of art which illustrate the miracle—for example, the marvel is portrayed in one of the stained glass windows of the cathedral in Dijon.

Reliquary containing the Sacred Host, gift of Duchess Isabella in 1454

Stained glass window of the Holy Chapel in the Cathedral of Dijon. In the first frame a priest presents the miraculous Host which remained intact until the French Revolution.

Old accurate reproduction of the Sacred Host of the Miracle of Dijon

Dijon, Host sent in 1433 by Pope Eugene IV to Phillip the Fair, Duke of Burgundy

In 1254 in Douai, a consecrated Host was unintentionally dropped to the ground while a priest was distributing Communion to the faithful. Immediately the priest bent down to pick up the Holy Eucharist, but the Host flew into the air and landed on the purificator. A little later, a wonderful Child appeared there, Whom all the faithful and religious present could see. Although more than 800 years have elapsed, even today one can still venerate the Host of the miracle. Every Thursday, many of the faithful gather in prayer before the miraculous Host in St. Pierre's Church in Douai.

Bonum universale de Apibus is the work written by an eyewitness of the miracle: the Dominican Father Thomas de Cantimpré, doctor of theology and "suffragan" Bishop of Cambrai. On Easter Day 1254 in St. Amatus' Church in Douai, a priest who was distributing Holy Communion unintentionally dropped a consecrated Host to the ground. Immediately he bent down to pick It up, but the Host flew up and landed on the purificator. A little later, a wonderful Child appeared there Whom all the faithful and religious present at the celebration could see. The news spread quickly, and the Bishop of Cambrai, Thomas de Cantimpré, immediately went to Douai to verify the facts in person. He described them in this manner: "I went to the dean of the church, followed by many faithful, and asked to see the miracle. The dean opened the small case in which he had reposed the Host of the miracle, but initially I didn't see anything special.

"I was conscious, though, that nothing could prevent me from seeing, as was true of the others, the Sacred Body. I didn't even have time to ask myself any questions along these lines, when I glanced at the Host and saw the face of Christ crowned with thorns, two

Tabernacle where the miraculous Host is kept

Exterior of the Church of St. Pierre in Douai

Monstrance containing the relic of the miraculous Host

Our Lady of Douai

1975. The pastor of the Church of St. Pierre shows the Host of 1254

drops of Blood descending down His forehead. Immediately I knelt, and weeping, began to thank God."

It is certain that by 1356, that is, a century after the apparition, every year on the Wednesday of Easter Week, a feast in memory of the miracle of the Blessed Sacrament was celebrated, and the document which records it indicates that this custom had already been in place a long time. The precious relic of the miracle was preserved and honored until the French Revolution. Then all traces of this marvel were lost for many years.

In October 1854, the pastor of St. Pierre's Church in Douai by chance discovered, underneath the Christ on the Altar of the Dead, a small wooden box containing a small Host, still white, but with damaged edges. A letter written in Latin gives witness: "I, the undersigned, canon of the distinguished collegial Church of St. Amatus, certify this to be the real and true Host of the holy miracle, which I removed from imminent danger of profanation.... I have placed the Host in this pyx and have left this witness, written by my own hand, for the faithful who will discover It in the future (January 5, 1793)."

On the vigil of the Feast of Pentecost, the monks of Faverney decided to expose the Blessed Sacrament for public adoration. During the night, a fire broke out which destroyed the altar and the sacred furnishings, but spared the monstrance containing the Sacred Host. The monstrance was retrieved after a few days, suspended in the air and perfectly intact. The miraculous Host is still kept today, and many are the pilgrims who hasten to venerate the miracle every year.

Stained glass window portraying the miracle

In the 17th century, Protestantism and Calvinism spread quickly in France because of the many material benefits conceded by the new religions to the nobility and clergy who left the Catholic Church. This placed the faith of many at risk and created great uncertainty, even in monasteries. In the city of Faverney there was a Benedictine abbey whose monks had departed far from the rule of their founder. The only thing they still held in high esteem was devotion to Our Lady of Notre-Dame la Blanche, known throughout the area. Through her intercession many miracles had taken place, including the return to life of two infants who had not yet been baptized.

In 1608, on the vigil of the Feast of Pentecost, the monks decided to prepare an altar for exposition and adoration of the Blessed Sacrament. The monstrance's lunette was very large, and because of this, they decided to put in two Hosts. When Vespers was finished, the monks left the monstrance exposed on the provisional altar.

The next morning, the sacristan opened the church and found it full of smoke, with the provisional altar completely reduced to ashes. He cried out, and immediately the religious and other people hastened to remove the ashes in the hope of finding some part of the monstrance. When the

Exposition of the Host of the miracle

Old print representing the miracle

Monstrance containing the relic of the miraculous Host

Interior of the church

Minor basilica, Favernay

smoke began to clear, they were astonished to see that the monstrance was suspended in the air. The multitude increased and crowded around to see the Eucharistic marvel in which the Hosts had remained unharmed despite the fire. The religious were astonished and, uncertain what to do, they asked counsel of the Capuchin friars of Vesoul. The friars immediately prepared a new altar over the burned one and celebrated Holy Mass. During the elevation of the Host, the monstrance slowly descended upon the new altar.

At the end of the canonical process, on July 10, the Archbishop of Besançon declared that the miracle was authentic, and on September 13, the Archbishop of Rodi, who was the nuncio in Brussels, told the story to Pope Paul V, who granted a Bull of Indulgence. The miracle rekindled the faith of many. In 1862, the Congregation of Rites authorized veneration of the miracle. In 1908 the third centenary of the miracle was solemnly commemorated with a National Eucharistic Congress. Even today it is possible to see and venerate the relic containing one of the two Hosts which remained unharmed. The other Host, which was donated to the church in Dole, was unfortunately destroyed by the revolutionaries in 1794.

The Eucharistic miracle of La Rochelle was the instantaneous cure of a boy, paralyzed and mute since the age of seven, who, when he received Holy Communion at Mass on Easter Sunday 1461, was completely healed of his paralysis and was able to speak again. The most authoritative document, which describes the miracle visually, is a painted manuscript still preserved today in the Cathedral of La Rochelle.

La Rochelle

The exterior of the church where the miraculous cure occurred

Black and white copy of one of the pages of the manuscript telling the story of the miracle

During Easter of 1461, Mrs. Jehan Leclerc brought her twelve-year-old son, Bertrand, to St. Bartholomew's Church. Due to a terrible fall, Bertrand had been paralyzed and mute since the age of seven. When the time for Holy Communion arrived, the boy indicated to his mother that he too wanted to receive Jesus in the Eucharist. Initially the priest did not want to give him Communion, because the boy was not able to go to Confession due to his muteness. The young man, however, continued to beg the priest, who, in the end, did permit him to receive the Eucharist.

The moment Bertrand received the Host, he began to feel shaken by a mysterious force. He was able to move and speak—he was cured. According to the document, which was written by hand immediately after the miraculous event, Bertrand's first words were, *"Adjutorium nostrum in nomine Domini!"* ("Our help is in the name of the Lord!") The most authoritative document, which visually describes this miracle, is the painted manuscript still preserved today in the Cathedral of La Rochelle.

There are two drops of the Blood of Our Lord Jesus Christ, collected on Calvary during the Passion, preserved in the Church of Neuvy-Saint-Sépulcre near Indre. They were brought to France in 1257 by Cardinal Eudes, who was returning from the Holy Land.

Reliquary of the Precious Blood

Interior of the basilica

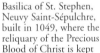

Basilica of St. Stephen, Neuvy Saint-Sépulchre, built in 1049, where the reliquary of the Precious Blood of Christ is kept

This relic of coagulated Blood is pure, not mixed with water or earth. Since 1257, the relic has been kept in this church which was built in the first half of the 10th century and was modeled on the Church of the Holy Sepulcher in Jerusalem. Numerous indulgences have been granted in honor of the sacred relic of the Most Precious Blood of Jesus. The Archbishop of Bruges, André Frémiot, founded the Confraternity of the Most Precious Blood in the year 1621 to spread devotion to this miracle. Two years later, Pope Gregory XV granted new indulgences to the faithful devoted to the Precious Blood. Every year on Easter Monday and on the first of July, a solemn Mass is celebrated and processions are organized to adore and honor the sacred relic. There have been many graces attributed to invoking the Precious Blood of Neuvy-Saint-Sépulcre.

In the Eucharistic miracle of Les Ulmes, during exposition of the Blessed Sacrament, in place of the Host there appeared the shape of a man with light brown hair falling over his shoulders, a luminous face, the hands crossed one over the other, and a white tunic covering the body. After close examination, the Bishop authorized devotion to this Eucharistic miracle. Even today in the church, the recess which contained the miraculous Host for more than 130 years can be seen. The Host was devoutly consumed by the vicar of Puy-Notre-Dame during the French Revolution for fear that the Blessed Sacrament might be profaned.

Old print representing the miracle, Paris

*O*n June 12, 1668, Saturday of the octave of Corpus Christi, in the small church of Les Ulmes, the Blessed Sacrament was exposed for public adoration. The church's pastor, Fr. Nicolas Nezan, began to incense the monstrance. As the hymn *Pange Lingua* was being sung, "when the stanza '*Verbum caro Panem verum*' was reached, the shape of a man appeared in the monstrance in place of the Host, with light brown hair falling over his shoulders, a luminous face, the hands crossed one over the other, and the body covered by a white tunic. This apparition lasted for more than a quarter of an hour, whether on the tabernacle where the Blessed Sacrament was exposed, or on the altar where the priest had moved the Blessed Sacrament to allow all those present to have a closer look."

On June 13, the pastor immediately sent a message regarding what had occurred to his Bishop, Henry Arnauld, who ordered an investigation. On June 25 a pastoral letter was published containing the "faithful description" of the marvel. Among the several subsequent works which copied the objective description contained in the letter, we remember that of the Dominican Father Gonet,

Parish church of Les Ulmes

who describes the event in Volume VIII of his work *Clypeus Theologiae,* first published in 1669 by the French editor Bertier.

The Bishop ordered news of this fact to be diffused widely. Thus three engravings were immediately commissioned: one by Edelynck, of the highest quality, which is still in Paris; one by Jean Bidault di Saumur; and lastly, one by the editor Ernoudi Parigi. Until the 18th century in the parish of Les Ulmes, every year the anniversary of the appari-

tion was solemnly celebrated. In 1901 the International Eucharistic Congress of Angers was celebrated in this parish, and in July 1933, during the National Eucharistic Congress, a complete study session was dedicated to the miracle of 1668. Even today in the church, the recess which for 130 years contained the miraculous Host can be seen. The Sacred Species were devoutly consumed during the French Revolution by the Vicar of Puy-Notre-Dame, who feared that the Blessed Sacrament would be profaned.

In 1533, thieves stole a ciborium containing consecrated Hosts from a church. The thieves then dumped the Hosts in a field. Although there was a heavy snowstorm, the Hosts were found a few days later in miraculously perfect condition. The numerous healings which followed this miracle and the tremendous popular devotion were not sufficient to protect the Hosts, which were destroyed by persons seeking to profane Them.

Window depicting the miracle

*I*n 1532, toward the end of December, thieves broke into the parish church of Marseille-en-Beauvais and stole a precious silver ciborium containing consecrated Hosts. The Hosts were abandoned under a large rock along the main street. On the first of January, Mr. Jean Moucque was walking down that street despite a heavy snowstorm. As he was walking, a rock on the side of the road caught his attention because it had no snow on it. When he lifted it, he was amazed to find the Hosts there, completely intact. He immediately told the pastor, Fr. Prothais, who, accompanied by many of the faithful, carried the Hosts back to the parish church.

A cross was placed at the spot where the Hosts had been found, and in order to accommodate the large number of devout faithful who came on pilgrimage, the Chapel of the Sacred Hosts was eventually built. The Lord worked many healings in this chapel. The historian Pierre Louvet describes some of these miracles in his history of the diocese of Beauvais. There was the extraordinary story of the priest, Fr. Jacques Sauvage, who was completely healed after being paralyzed

and having lost his ability to speak. Mr. d'Autreche, blind from birth, gained his sight.

Despite all these graces given by God, the Count-Bishop of Beauvais, Odet de Coligny, converted to Calvinism and married Elizabeth of Hauteville. Before publicly renouncing his faith, he ordered the Hosts to be consumed. However, the Chapel of the Sacred Hosts still stands, and every year on January 2nd, a solemn Mass is celebrated in honor of the miracle of 1533.

During Easter of 1290, a non-believer who hated the Faith and did not believe in the Real Presence of Christ in the Eucharist gained possession of a consecrated Host with the intention of desecrating It. He stabbed the Host and threw It into boiling water. The Host miraculously rose out of the water into the air right in front of the man, who was terrified. He put the Host into a bowl belonging to a pious woman, who immediately brought the Host to her pastor. The ecclesiastical authorities, the people and the king decided to transform the desecrator's house into a chapel where the Sacred Host was kept until It was destroyed during the Revolution.

Window of the Church of St. Etienne representing the miracle

*T*here are numerous documents testifying to the events of this miracle. The Italian historian Giovanni Villani, in Book VII, Chapter 136 of his celebrated *History of Florence,* briefly recounts all the principal facts of the miracle. An in-depth study of the sources was undertaken by Mrs. Moreau-Rendu in a work entitled *A Paris, Rue des Jardins,* published in 1954 with a preface by Bishop Touzé who was the Auxiliary Bishop of Paris. The author, after a rigorous examination of the documents, declared with confidence the authenticity of the facts. The best-known version of the story is found in the *History of the Church of Paris* written by the French Archbishop Rupp, who tells of the Eucharistic miracle of Paris in the pages dedicated to the episcopate of Simon Matifas de Busay, who held the see of St. Denis from 1290 to 1304:

"On Easter Sunday, April 2, 1290, a man named Jonathas, who hated the Catholic Faith and did not believe in the Real Presence of Christ in the Holy Eucharist, gained possession of a consecrated Host.

"The man stabbed the Host with a knife, and the Host began to bleed. The Blood filled the container in

Demolition of the Church of Saint-Jean-en-Grève.
Pierre-Antoine Demachy (1797)

Miniature representing the sacrilege (16th century),
kept in the National Archives

The Church of St. Etienne du Mont

which he had placed the Host. Panic-stricken, the man decided to throw the Blessed Sacrament into the fire, but the Host miraculously rose out of the fire. Desperate, he then threw the Eucharist into boiling water, and the Host suddenly rose from the water into the air and then took on the form of a crucifix. Finally, he deposited the Holy Eucharist in the bowl of a parishioner of Saint-Jean-en-Grève, who brought the Blessed Sacrament to her parish priest. Over the centuries, the Host remained in a small reliquary in the Church of Saint-Jean. During the French Revolution the precious relic was lost without a trace."

Here are some other equally significant facts: King Phillip the Fair's confiscation of Jonathas' house, called "The House of Miracles," which was registered in a bill of sale from 1291; the transformation of the house into an oratory after the bull obtained from Pope Boniface VIII; the name of the street, "Rue du Dieu bouilli" ("The Street of God-boiled") given by the people of Paris to the "Rue des Jardins"; and the Eucharistic celebration in the Chapel des Billettes of the Office of Reparation on the second Sundays of Advent and Lent.

Desperate, he threw the Host into boiling water and It rose into the air, taking on the form of a crucifix.

The Triumph of the Eucharist

The interior of the cloister of the church des Billetes

Cloister des Billetes which has today become a Protestant church

Sculptures of the events
of the miracle

Chapel of the Catechisms, Church of St. Etienne

A chalice in which a consecrated Host had been placed was completely melted after a devastating fire in the parish church. The only thing remaining of the chalice was its base, on which had formed a tin bubble; underneath this, the Host was found completely intact. The miraculous Host was consumed the day afterwards, but there are still in existence many documents which testify to this miracle. Among these documents are the windows of the church in Pressac which depict the different phases of the miracle.

PORTRAIT DV MIRACLE ARIVÉ A PRESSAC LE IEVDY ABSOLV SECOND IOVR D'AVRIL 1643

A *Poincts representans le voile brûlé.*
B *Ombre representant la couppe fondue.*
C *Cendre, auec feu procedant de l'incendie.*
D *Hostie conseruée soubs jouët la cendre.*
E *Fons du calice resté de la couppe fondue, noira de l'embrasement*
F *Larmes d'stain fondu attachées au pommeau du pied du calice*
G *Larmes d'estain fondu attachées au pied du calice.*
H *Corporalier conserué de l'incendie.*

*T*his miracle occurred on Holy Thursday 1643. After assisting at Mass and receiving Communion, the people of the town returned to their occupations and the priest placed the chalice back on the repository. This was near the altar dedicated to the Blessed Virgin and was supported by four pillars of wood surrounding a marble slab, on top of which was a corporal. Behind the altar there was a depiction of a Eucharistic scene. A veil covered the chalice, and two large candles were lit at the foot of the repository. It was mid-day, and the sacristan closed the church.

Two hours later, those nearby noticed thick black smoke coming from the church windows. Since the windows had been inadvertently left open, this probably fanned the candle flames and accelerated the fire. The people called the sacristan to unlock the doors, and they all entered to assess the damage. The repository and the painting were destroyed. What was left were the marble slab, the corporal, and the base of the chalice. The report would later say that almost the entire chalice was transformed into "drops of tin."

On the remnant of the chalice was a bubble of tin under which the Host

Church of St. Justus, Pressac

Foot of the miraculous chalice

Carved mask on the door of the Church of St. Justus at Pressac

Depiction of the chalice as it appeared after the Miracle of Pressac next to the account written by François du Theil, curate of Availles-Limouzine, in the year 1643

was found completely intact, having withstood the flames and the melted metal. The vicar, Fr. Simon Sauvage, hurried to the scene of the miracle and carried the melted chalice to the main altar for all to see. The Host, light red around the edges, was consumed the next morning during the Divine Office of Good Friday. (We should remember that the Liturgy back then required that only one of the consecrated Hosts should be reserved in the ciborium after the Holy Thursday Mass and placed in a chalice covered by a simple veil.)

The Abbot of Availles-Limouzine, François du Theil, recorded all the tes-timonies and gave them to the Bishop of Poitiers, Henri Louis Chastagnier de la Roche Posay, who authorized the cult of the miracle with a solemn act which states: "The Sacred Mysteries are incomprehensible, if the splendor of grace does not illumine the spirit in order to elevate it to the highest understanding of the wondrous effects of God's power. So that all men might adore Him to Whom it is due, God's ineffable goodness is manifested at times in extraordinary ways, work-ing miracles in the Church in order to confirm the Catholic Faith and to confound the errors of the unfaithful spirits."

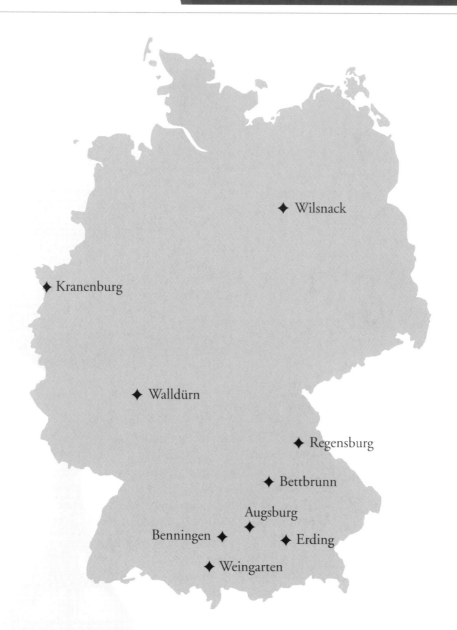

♦ Wilsnack

♦ Kranenburg

♦ Walldürn

♦ Regensburg

♦ Bettbrunn

Augsburg
Benningen ♦   ♦   ♦ Erding

♦ Weingarten

The Eucharistic miracle of Augsburg is known locally as *Wunderbarlichen Gutes* – "The Miraculous Good." It is described in numerous books and historical documents which can be consulted in Augsburg's public library. A stolen Host was transformed into bleeding Flesh. Over the course of the centuries, several scientific analyses of the Sacred Host have been carried out. These have always confirmed that human Flesh and Blood are present. Today the Convent of the *Heileg Kreuz* (Holy Cross) is under the care of the Dominican Fathers.

In 1194, a woman from Augsburg who was particularly devoted to the Blessed Sacrament hid a Host in her handkerchief, took It home and placed It in a wax container inside a cupboard. (In those days it was very difficult to find tabernacles in churches for Eucharistic adoration. Only in 1264, with the introduction of the Feast of Corpus Christi, did such devotion become commonplace.)

Five years passed, and on the 11th of May 1199, the woman, tormented by remorse, confessed what she had done to the superior of the Convent of the Heilig Kreuz, Fr. Berthold, who had her bring the Host back. The priest opened the wax container and saw that the Host had been transformed into bleeding Flesh. The Host appeared "divided into two parts connected by thin threads of bleeding Flesh." Fr. Berthold immediately went to Bishop Udalskalk, who ordered that the miraculous Host be "transferred, accompanied by the clergy and people, to the cathedral and exhibited in a crystal monstrance for public worship."

The miracle continued: the Host began to grow and swell, and this phenomenon was seen by all from Easter Sunday until the Feast of St. John the Baptist.

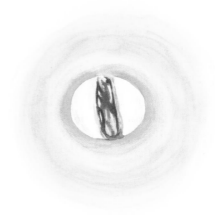

Reliquary containing the Host of the miracle, known as *Wunderbarlichen Gutes*

Convent of the Heilig Kreuz (Holy Cross), Augsburg

Following this, Bishop Udalskalk had the Host brought back to the Convent of the Heilig Kreuz and proclaimed that "in memory of such a memorable and extraordinary event," there should be a special feast each year in honor of the holy relic.

In 1200, Count Rechber gave the Augustinian Fathers a rectangular chest of silver with an opening in front for the placement of the miraculous Host. Besides the Eucharistic miracle, other extraordinary incidents took place, such as the apparition above the Host of Baby Jesus dressed in white with a radiant face, His forehead encir-

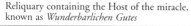

cled by a crown of gold, the bleeding of the church's crucifix, and the apparition of Jesus blessing the assembly.

In 1216 the village of Benningen was the scene of a Eucharistic miracle in which the Host bled. A few years later, in 1221, the citizens of Benningen began construction of a chapel in honor of this miracle. The chapel is known as *Riedkapelle zum Hochwürdigen Gut*. From 1674 to 1718 the *Riedkapelle* was rebuilt and enlarged to accommodate the large number of pilgrims. Each year during the Feast of Corpus Christi, the parish of Benningen goes in procession to the *Riedkapelle* to commemorate the miracle.

An old document of 1216 tells the story of two millers who, for years, had been at odds with each other. One day, one of them, exasperated by yet another argument, after receiving Holy Communion, stole a consecrated Host which he then hid between his neighbor's millstones with the intent of slandering him. On the feast of St. Gregory, the Host began to bleed so profusely that the whole village and the Bishop learned about it. The blasphemous miller repented and confessed his misdeed.

The paintings in the chapel built in honor of the miracle were executed by Johann Friedrich Sichelbein to illustrate the story. The portrait above the altar shows the Bishop of Augsburg, Frederick, who deposited the Host in a precious container in St. Martin's Church in Memmingen. Over the course of the centuries, unfortunately, the precious relic was lost.

For a long time, it was believed that the paintings adorning the chapel were copies of those exhibited in the museum of the Ottobeuren Monastery. Only during the restoration of 1987 was it discovered that the paintings were the originals. On the wooden ceiling there are frescoes illustrating the Passion of Christ and scenes from the Old and New Testaments.

Inside the *Riedkapelle*

Johann Friederich Silbelbein (1640). *Procession of the Miraculous Host*

The external façade of the *Riedkapelle*

In the village of Bettbrunn, a pious farmer, in an excess of zeal, stole a consecrated Host which he brought to his farm in Viehbrunn. One day, the Host accidentally fell to the ground, but despite all efforts, no one could pick It up. Finally the Bishop of Regensburg intervened. He was able to pick up the Host only after promising the Lord that he would build a church in honor of the Blessed Sacrament. Reports of the miracle spread rapidly and attracted a large number of pilgrims.

Holy Savior Church, Bettbrunn

The village of Bettbrunn and the present-day Church of the Holy Savior owe their existence to a Eucharistic miracle which took place in 1125. Where the town and church now stand, there was once only a small farm called Viehbrunn; next to it was a well that was used to water the livestock. The owner was a man who was deeply devoted to the Most Blessed Sacrament. This man lived an hour and a half away from the parish church of Tholling, and he was not always able to attend Mass.

Because of his zeal, he decided to solve this problem by stealing a consecrated Host and taking the Blessed Sacrament home with him. The farmer took the stick he always carried with him and made an opening on top, into which he placed the Sacred Host. Every day, when the livestock were resting, he stuck his stick into the ground and knelt before the Blessed Sacrament for many hours. For several months, the man continued in this manner until one day, without thinking, he impulsively threw the stick with the Blessed Sacrament at a herd that had strayed too far.

The Host fell to the ground and the farmer, deeply saddened, bent down to pick up the Blessed Sacrament. Every

Interior of Holy Savior Church

Old image of Holy Savior Church

The faithful on pilgrimage to Bettbrunn

attempt to lift the Host proved futile. When he had tried everything else, the farmer went to call the parish priest of Tholling. But the priest was also unable to pick up the Blessed Sacrament. Finally they approached Bishop Hartwich of Regensburg, who immediately went to the place of the miracle with all his clergy. Only when he had promised to build a chapel there did the Bishop succeed in picking up the Host. In 1125, the chapel was completed and the precious relic was kept there until a fire destroyed everything in 1330. The chapel was later rebuilt, and in its interior they placed one of the pillars which had been saved from the fire.

On Holy Thursday 1417, a peasant stole a consecrated Host, which, in the course of his journey, slipped from his hands and flew up into the air. He tried in vain to catch It. Only when the Bishop directly intervened was the Host retrieved. A chapel was immediately built on the site where the miracle occurred. Many cures and wonders have been attributed to veneration of this miracle.

A poor peasant in Erding could find no way to improve his economic status although he worked many hours each day. His neighbor who did the same work, on the other hand, lived prosperously. One day the peasant asked his neighbor how he had succeeded in earning so much, and the man confided to him that his success was owed to the fact that he kept the Blessed Sacrament in his house. The poor peasant, ignorant in the faith, thought that the Blessed Sacrament was a type of amulet, and decided to imitate his neighbor. He went to Mass on Holy Thursday and, after having received Communion, hid the Host in a cloth and left the church. Almost immediately, however, he regretted his action, so he decided to bring the Host back. Along the way, however, It slipped out of his hand and rose into the air. He searched for It everywhere, to no avail.

Terrified, he ran to inform the pastor, who immediately went to the spot where the Host had disappeared. As soon as he arrived the priest saw the Sacred Particle resting on a clump of dirt, emitting a bright light. He reached for the Sacred Host, which again flew up into the air and disappeared. The priest told the Bishop, who wanted to

Interior of the sanctuary

Relic of the Precious Blood

Sanctuary of the Most Precious Blood

go in person to the site of the miracle. Once again the Host flew up into the air. The Bishop and the townspeople then decided to build a chapel in honor of the Eucharistic wonder. Such crowds of pilgrims flocked there that in 1675, the local authorities decided to construct a new and larger sanctuary in the baroque style. On Sept. 19, 1677, Bishop Kaspar Künner of Freising blessed the new church, which was dedicated to the Most Precious Blood. Various relics were brought to the sanctuary, among which was a relic of the Most Precious Blood of Christ. Since 1992 the sanctuary has been under the care of the monks of St. Paul of the Desert.

In 1280, in the small town of Kranenburg in the district of Kleve, there was a Eucharistic miracle known by the name of "Wonder of the Miraculous Crucifix." A consecrated Host was thrown near a tree by a shepherd who was not able to swallow It because of an illness. Later, the tree was cut in half, and a perfectly-carved crucifix fell to the ground. On the spot where the crucifix was found, a church was built. That church is still there today, and each year numerous pilgrims come to visit it. Popes and Bishops have always encouraged veneration of the miraculous crucifix, granting privileges and indulgences, most recently during the Holy Year 2000.

*M*any documents describe this miracle which took place in 1280. A shepherd from Kranenburg, after receiving Holy Communion, was unable to swallow the Host and threw It against a tree in his garden. He was plagued with remorse over the incident and decided to tell his parish priest. The priest hastened to the place of the evil deed to try to find the Host, but the search proved fruitless.

A few years later, the tree was cut down and split into two pieces. Right after it was cut down, a perfectly-carved crucifix fell out of the tree. The report of the crucifix which had "grown from a consecrated Host" spread rapidly from town to town. The Bishops of Cologne and the Count of Kleve took a direct interest in the miracle, and pilgrims began to come in large numbers. In 1408, the citizens of Kranenburg began construction of a church in honor of the miracle. The church was completed around 1444 and represents one of the most significant examples of Gothic architectural style in the lower Rhine area. Popes and Bishops have always promoted veneration of the

Relic of the miraculous crucifix

Fifteenth-century document describing the miracle preserved at the church

Procession held every year on September 14 in honor of the miracle

Detail of the relic

Church of St. Peter and Paul where the precious relic is kept

miraculous crucifix, granting privileges and indulgences, the most recent of which were granted in the year 2000.

In the Eucharistic miracle of Regensburg, a priest was assailed by doubts concerning the Real Presence of Jesus in the Eucharist during Mass. At the moment of the elevation of the chalice, the wooden crucifix above the tabernacle came to life, and the Lord slowly extended His arms to the priest, took the chalice from his hands, and held it up for the adoration of the faithful.

The crucifix of the miracle

*O*n Holy Thursday, March 25, 1255, a priest from Ratisbonne was taking Viaticum to a dying man when, upon entering the city, he suddenly found himself before a stream, overflowing because of an unexpected storm. A simple wood plank had been placed across the stream to allow travelers to cross. While crossing it, the priest slipped and dropped the ciborium containing the consecrated Hosts. That same day, the priest, the faithful, and the civil authorities decided to construct a chapel as an act of reparation on the site of the accident. On September 8, 1255, Bishop Albert consecrated the chapel in honor of the Savior, to which the Blessed Sacrament was carried in solemn procession. From that moment on the sanctuary was visited by numerous faithful.

Two years later an extraordinary event confirmed the holiness of the place. A priest was celebrating Mass in the little chapel when he was struck by doubts regarding the Real Presence of Jesus in the Eucharist. He delayed, therefore, in elevating the chalice, and suddenly heard a slight noise coming from the altar. From the wooden crucifix above the altar, the Lord slowly extended

Old print depicting the miracle

His arms to the priest, took the chalice from his hands and held it up for the adoration of the faithful. The priest, repentant, fell to his knees and begged forgiveness for having doubted. The Lord returned the chalice to him as a sign of pardon.

The miraculous crucifix is still preserved to this day in the nearby town of Regensburg, and many of the faithful go there every year on pilgrimage.

Original chapel of the miracle

One of the most complete documents regarding the Eucharistic miracle of Walldürn, Germany, in the year 1330, is the one written by the monk Hoffius in 1589. During the Mass, a priest accidentally knocked over the chalice of consecrated wine, which turned into Blood and formed an image of the Crucified Christ on the corporal. The relic of the corporal stained with Blood is preserved today on the side altar in the minor basilica of St. George in Walldürn. Every year, several thousand pilgrims visit Walldürn to venerate the sacred relic.

The Crucified Christ is clearly distinguished under ultraviolet lighting

Fr. Heinrich Otto was celebrating Mass one day when he accidentally knocked over the chalice containing the Blood of Christ. Immediately upon spilling, the Precious Blood formed on the corporal a red image of the Crucified Christ, surrounded by eleven identical images of the Head of Christ crowned with thorns. The priest did not have the courage to reveal the miracle, and for many years he kept the corporal hidden under the altar. It was only at the point of death that in confession he told the story to the priest and gave him the corporal.

From the beginning, the reliquary of the corporal has been much venerated, and many conversions and miraculous recoveries are attributed to it. Pope Eugene IV confirmed the miracle in 1445 and granted some indulgences. The miracle became famous all over Europe and for centuries was depicted by many artists.

The present basilica was constructed between 1698 and 1728 by Franz Lothar von Schonborn, Archbishop of Mainz. In 1962, Pope John XXIII elevated the church to the status of minor basilica. Augustinian monks have been in charge of the basilica since 1938.

Interior of the church   Church of St. George

Banner in the Church of St. George on which the miracle is presented

Fr. Augustine presents the miraculous corporal to pilgrims

Procession in honor of the miracle

Church of St. George

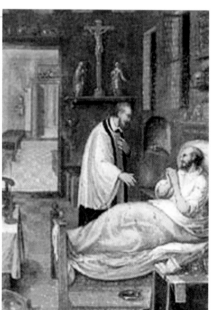

Fr. Otto hides the miraculous corporal. This painting is in the Church of St. George and was painted in 1732

For more than 900 years a relic of the Most Precious Blood of Jesus has been venerated at the Benedictine monastery in Weingarten. According to many historians, the soldier Longinus had carried the relic of the Precious Blood of Christ to Mantua. Later, It was divided into several portions and given to various rulers of the era, the most famous of whom was Charlemagne, and to different Popes.

Relic of the Most Precious Blood

A relic of the Most Precious Blood is found in Weingarten. According to an ancient document, in the year 1055, Emperor Henry III of the Franks was given part of the precious relic. Henry subsequently left It as an inheritance to Count Baldwin of Flanders, who in turn gave It to his daughter Judith.

When Guelph IV of Bavaria sought Judith as his spouse, she gave him the precious relic, which he himself later gave to the Benedictines at Weingarten, headed at the time by Abbot Wilichon.

The solemn ceremony took place on March 4, 1094. For this reason the Benedictine abbey received numerous indulgences from various Popes, so that this church became a religious center of extraordinary importance.

Every year, a ceremony known as The Ride (or Procession) of the Blood, in honor of the relic, is organized at Weingarten. This is a parade of nearly 3,000 horses, ridden by representatives of the individual parishes and by the clergy of individual churches.

Procession in honor of the precious relic

Relic of a nail from the Cross, Kunsthistorisches Museum in Vienna

Relic of the True Cross which is preserved in Rome in the Basilica of the Holy Cross in Jerusalem

Pope Pius II venerates the precious Relic

The relic of the Most Precious Blood is preserved in the Church of St. Martin in Weingarten

Every year a
ceremony known
as The Ride
(or Procession)
of the Blood,
in honor of the
relic, is organized
at Weingarten.

The relic of the Precious Blood (17th century). City Hall in Weingarten

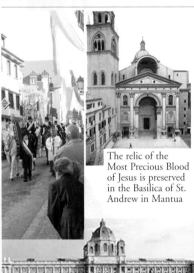

The relic of the Most Precious Blood of Jesus is preserved in the Basilica of St. Andrew in Mantua

A letter from 1278, dated March 1, in which Albert, abbot of the Benedictine Monastery of St. Andrew in Mantua, confirms the Mantuan origin of the relic of the Precious Blood of Jesus, preserved in the monastery at Weingarten

Relics of the Precious Blood, Mantua

Kunsthistorisches Museum, Vienna

An old painting depicting the Ride (the Transport or Procession) of the Most Precious Blood held in Weingarten

Procession in honor of the Precious Blood at Mantua

Monstrances containing some relics of the Passion of Christ, Kunsthistorishces Museum, Vienna

Mantua and Weingarten are sister cities

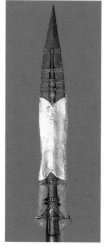

Relic of the Sacred Lance with which the Roman soldier struck the side of Jesus. Kunsthistorisches Museum, Vienna

Reliquary containing the soil on which the Most Precious Blood of Christ fell from the Cross, Czestochowa, Poland

In 1383, a terrible fire destroyed the village of Wilsnack. Among the ruins of the parish church were found three completely intact Hosts which bled repeatedly. Pilgrims began to go there in great numbers, and a church was built in honor of the miracle. Veneration of this miracle was approved by two bulls of Pope Eugene IV in 1447.

Count Dietrich von Wenckstern recovers his sight after repenting for having doubted the truth of the Bleeding Hosts

*I*n August 1383, the village of Wilsnack was sacked, robbed and set afire by a knight named Heinrich von Bulow. Among the ruins of the parish church were found three perfectly intact Hosts from which Blood flowed. After the bleeding Hosts were found, numerous miracles began to take place. For example, the knight Dietrich von Wenckstern, who doubted the bleeding of the Hosts, lost his vision, which was restored only when he repented of having doubted the authenticity of the miracle.

The news spread rapidly, and by 1384 the Bishop of Havelburg had confirmed the miracle of the "bleeding" Hosts of Wilsnack. Pope Urban VI contributed an endowment for reconstruction of the church, to which were added offerings by the Archbishop of Magdeburg and the Bishops of Brandenburg, Havelberg, and Levus. Until the 1500s, Wilsnack became one of the most important pilgrimage places in Europe. Thanks to numerous offerings left by pilgrims who came to venerate the miraculous Hosts, it was

Memorial honoring the three Miraculous Hosts of Wilsnack

Church of St. Nicholas in Wilsnack

Interior of the church

hyr werth dat godeßhuß tho Wilsnagt mit gr ter gnade vnde aflath begiffriger.

hyr kömeth de kerkhere vnde suth syne kerke vnde dat dorp vorbranth.

Old prints depicting the events of the miracle

possible to finance the construction of the enormous Church of St. Nicholas, dedicated to the miracle. Even today the church offers one of the most important examples of the Gothic style in fired brick typical of northern Germany. The monstrance containing the relics of the three Hosts was destroyed in a fire in 1522. However, numerous written testimonials regarding the miracle survive, along with works of art depicting it.

◆ Chirattakonam

This Eucharistic miracle took place recently, on May 5, 2001, in Trivandrum, India. In the Host there appeared the face of a man similar to that of Christ crowned with thorns. His Beatitude Cyril Mar Baselice, Archbishop of the diocese of Trivandrum, wrote regarding this prodigy: "[...] For us believers, what we have seen is something that we have always believed [...]. If our Lord is speaking to us by giving us this sign, certainly it requires a response from us." The monstrance containing the miraculous Host is still kept in the church.

Fr. Johnson Karoor, pastor of the church where this Eucharistic miracle took place, recounts in his deposition: "On April 28, 2001, in the parish church of St. Mary of Chirattakonam, we began the Novena to St. Jude Thaddeus as we do every year. At 8:49 AM, I exposed the Most Blessed Sacrament in the monstrance for public adoration. After a few minutes I saw what appeared to be three dots on the Holy Eucharist. I then stopped praying and began to look at the monstrance, also inviting the faithful to admire the three dots. I then asked the faithful to remain in prayer and reposed the monstrance in the tabernacle. On April 30th, I celebrated Holy Mass, and on the following day I left for Trivandrum.

"On Saturday morning, the 5th of May 2001, I opened the church for the usual liturgical celebrations. I vested for Mass and went to open the tabernacle to see what had happened to the Eucharist in the monstrance. I immediately noted in the Host a figure like that of a human face. I was deeply moved and asked the faithful to kneel and begin praying. I thought I alone could see the face, so I asked the altar server what he noticed in the monstrance. He answered: 'I see the figure of a man.' I noticed that the rest of the faithful were also looking intently at the monstrance.

"We began adoration, and as the minutes went by, the image became clearer and clearer. I did not have the courage to say

His Beatitude Cyril Mar Baselice, Archbishop of the diocese of Trivandrum

Monstrance containing the Host in which the image appeared

anything, and I began to weep. During adoration, we have the practice of reading a passage from Holy Scriptures. The reading of the day was the one from Chapter 20 in the Gospel of John, which narrates the story of when the Risen Jesus appears to St. Thomas and asks him to look at His wounds. I was only able to say a few words in my homily, and, having to leave for the nearby parish of Kokkodu to celebrate Mass, I immediately summoned a photographer to take pictures of the Holy Eucharist with the human face on it. After two hours all the photos were developed; with the passing of time, the face in every photo became clearer and clearer."

Saint-André de la Réunion ◆

On January 26, 1902, in the parish church of Saint-André, a city on the Island of La Réunion (a French colony), Abbot Henry Lacombe, the church's pastor, witnessed a miracle which he himself would recount to thousands of people during the Eucharistic Congress of Angoulême (1904), as well as to a group of priests gathered for a retreat in the town of Périgueux. The face of Jesus appeared on the Host and was witnessed for many hours by thousands of people.

et us examine Abbot Lacombe's account: "It was January 26, 1902. We were celebrating Forty Hours. The Blessed Sacrament was exposed in the tabernacle. I began the Mass. After the elevation, at the moment of the Our Father, I lifted my eyes toward the Host and saw a bright halo around the rays of the monstrance. I continued to recite the prayers of the Mass with great agitation in my soul, which I tried to overcome. When the moment for Communion came, again I looked toward the monstrance. This time I saw a human face, with lowered eyes and a crown of thorns on the forehead. What moved me the most was the dolorous expression on the face. The eyelashes were long and thick. I tried not to let my inner turmoil show. After Mass, I went to the sacristy and summoned the older children from the choir to go to the altar and closely observe the monstrance.

"The children raced back and told me: 'Father, we see a man's head in the Host. It is the good Lord revealing Himself!' I understood then that the vision was authentic. A young man of 16, Adam de Villiers, who had studied in France, also arrived. I said to him as well: 'Go into the church and see if you notice anything extraordinary in the tabernacle.' The young student went to the church and returned immediately,

Réunion Island

Print representing the prodigy

saying: 'Father, it is the good Lord who is appearing in the Host. I see His divine face.' From that moment on, all my doubts disappeared. Little by little the entire town gathered in the church to see the miracle. Journalists and people from the capital of Saint Denis also arrived. The face on the Host suddenly became animated and the crown of thorns disappeared. I took every possible precaution, and fearing effects from the rays of light, I had all the candles extinguished and the shutters closed. The phenomenon became clearer. In fact, in the darkness the lines of that face began to glow. Among the visitors there was a young artist who faithfully reproduced the face in the Host. Some of the visitors even brought magnifying glasses, but there was no need to use them. Later, the vision changed again and a crucifix appeared which covered the entire Host from top to bottom. After Benediction and the recital of the *Tantum Ergo*, the vision disappeared."

Eucharistic Miracles of
ITALY

Valvasone
Gruaro

Turin
Asti

Dronero
Canosio

Ferrara

Rimini
Florence
Bagno di Romagna
Volterra
Rosano
Siena
Morrovalle
Macerata
Assisi
Offida
Bolsena
Cascia

Rome
Alatri
Lanciano
Veroli

Trani

Patierno
Scala
Cava dei Tirreni

Mogoro
San Mauro la Bruca

In Alatri's Cathedral of St. Paul the Apostle, there is kept even today the reliquary of a Eucharistic miracle that occurred in 1228 when a fragment of the Host turned into Flesh. A young woman, in an effort to regain the love of her sweetheart, consulted a sorceress who ordered her to steal a consecrated Host to make a love potion. During Mass, the young woman hid a Host in a cloth. But when she got home, she realized that the Host had been transformed into bleeding Flesh. There is extensive documentation of this miracle, including a bull by Pope Gregory IX.

Paintings in the cathedral of Alatri which illustrate the various stages of the miracle

The most authoritative testimony regarding this miracle is found in the bull *Fraternitas tuae* (March 13, 1228) written by Pope Gregory IX in response to Bishop John V of Alatri. The text reads: "Gregory, Bishop and Servant of the Servants of God, to our Venerable Brother Bishop of Alatri, health and apostolic benediction. We have received your letter, dearest brother, in which you inform us of a certain young girl misguided by the wicked advice of an evil woman; after having received from the priest the Most Holy Body of Christ, she kept the Sacred Host in her mouth until she was able to conceal It in a cloth. Three days later, she discovered the same Body which she had received in the form of bread transformed into flesh, as anyone can verify with his own eyes. Because both women have humbly revealed this to you, you desire our opinion regarding the punishment to be imposed upon them. First, we must give thanks with all our strength to Him Who, though He always operates in marvelous ways, at times repeats miracles and produces new wonders so that, by strengthening our faith in the truths of the Catholic Church, sustaining our hope, and re-igniting our charity, He calls to sinners, converts evildoers, and confounds the wickedness of heretics.

The chapel where the enfleshed Host is exposed

Cathedral of Saint Paul in Alatri

Monstrance where the relic of the miracle is kept

Chapel inside the cathedral where the reliquary of the miracle is kept

Bull *Fraternitas Tuae* of Pope Gregory IX

Letter of the rector of Santa Maria alle Terme, dated March 22, 1888, in which he gives thanks for the gift of part of the relic of the enfleshed Host conserved in Alatri

Detail of the relic

"Thus, dearest brother, by means of this apostolic letter, we ordain that you inflict a milder punishment on the young woman, whom we hold to have done this more out of weakness than from malice, especially because it can be believed that she has sufficiently repented in confessing her sin. To the instigator, who by her perversion urged the young woman to commit sacrilege, apply those disciplinary measures that we believe opportune to leave to your judgment. Tell her that she should visit the nearest bishops and humbly confess her crime, imploring pardon with devout submission."

The Pope interpreted this episode as a sign against the widespread heresies

The 750th anniversary of the miracle was solemnly celebrated in 1978. For the occasion, a medal was coined which on the front shows an image of Pope Gregory IX with the Bull, and on the back, the façade of the cathedral with the Host above it

regarding the Real Presence of Jesus in the Eucharist and pardoned the two repentant women. A commemorative medal was coined on the 750th anniversary of the miracle; one side showed the front of the cathedral with the enfleshed Host above it, while the other showed a bust of Pope Gregory IX with the papal bull.

In both of the Eucharistic miracles of Asti, real Blood gushed from consecrated Hosts, and there are numerous documents confirming these events. In the first miracle, Bishop Scipione Roero of Asti had a notarized act drawn up immediately, and on November 6, 1535, Pope Paul III granted a plenary indulgence to anyone who visited the Church of San Secondo on the anniversary of the miraculous event.

Interior of the Collegiate Church of San Secondo

On July 25, 1535, while celebrating Mass at the main altar of the Collegiate Church of San Secondo at about 7 o'clock in the morning, a holy priest by the name of Domenico Occelli broke the Host and noticed that, along the entire break, It was turning red with living Blood. Three drops fell into the chalice and a fourth one remained on the edge of the Host. At first, Fr. Domenico continued to celebrate Mass. But when he broke off a portion of the Host to place it in the chalice, more Blood came out of the Host. He could not believe his eyes, and he turned to the people,

inviting them to come to the altar and observe the miracle. When the priest was about to consume the Host, the Blood disappeared and the Host regained its natural whiteness.

These are the facts as described in the official report sent by Bishop Scipione Roero of Asti to the Holy See and reproduced in the apostolic brief of November 6, 1535. In this apostolic brief Pope Paul III granted a plenary indulgence to those "who visit the saint's church on the day commemorating the miracle and recite three Our Fathers and three Hail Marys for the

Oil painting on canvas (by an unknown 17th century painter) depicting the Eucharistic miracle that took place in the Collegiate Church of San Secondo in 1535. The painting is kept in the chapel of the miracle

Collegiate Church of San Secondo in Asti

G. Badarello (toward the end of the 17th century), Collegiate Church of San Secondo, altar of the crucifix or of the miracle

intentions of the Holy Father."

According to another document, reproduced on a marble tablet, on that occasion some heretical soldiers, seeing the miracle, converted to the faith. In those days, Asti was under the dominion of Emperor Charles V, and many of his troops were living in the city. This account, besides being found in the Vatican archives from which a copy was made in 1884 at the request of Canon Longo, is also found in the book of the Company of the Most Blessed Sacrament, which was founded in the Collegiate Church of San Secondo in 1519. Other testimonies are a 16th-century painting in the Chapel of the Crucifix depicting the miracle, as well as an inscription on marble with the words: *Hic ubi Christus Ex Sacro pane Effuso sanguine Exteram vi traxit fidem Astensem roboravit*—"Here, having shed Blood from the Holy Bread, Christ drew foreigners to the faith and strengthened that of the people of Asti."

The second miracle took place in the old chapel of the Pious Association of Milliavacca and was documented by numerous testimonies gathered by a notary public and signed by the priest and eminent ecclesiastical and lay authorities.

The chalice of the miracle is kept in the Cathedral of Asti, in the chapel dedicated to St. Philip Neri

On the morning of May 10, 1718, Father Francesco Scotto went to the Milliavacca (a boarding school) to celebrate Holy Mass. It was about 8 o'clock. The church was divided into two parts, the front where outsiders could gather, and the back behind the altar, reserved for the boarding students. In front of the altar, there was only the notary Scipione Alessandro Ambrogio, who was the Bishop's chancellor and treasurer of the institute. The boarding students were in the back. When the priest elevated the consecrated Host, Dr. Ambrogio realized that It was divided into two parts. As soon as the priest elevated the chalice, the man, convinced that a broken Host was not valid matter, went toward the altar to tell the priest, and immediately ran into the sacristy to get another host. In the meantime the priest lifted the consecrated Host with his finger and found that It was really broken in half, and to his great surprise, the broken edges of the two parts were stained with Blood. The chalice's base and cup also had drops of Blood on them, and little stains of Blood were also present on the corporal.

In the meantime Dr. Ambrogio had arrived with a new host and realized that the original Host was bleeding. He immediately began to weep. All those present saw the miracle. The notary ran to call Fr. Argenta, the school's confessor, the theologian Vaglio, and

Detail of the base of the chalice of the miracle of Opera Pia Milliavacca

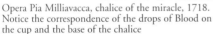

Opera Pia Milliavacca, chalice of the miracle, 1718. Notice the correspondence of the drops of Blood on the cup and the base of the chalice

Cathedral of Asti

Ferrero the penitentiary, who also witnessed the miracle.

At the same time, other priests and three doctors arrived. Drs. Argenta, Volpini and Vercellone gave sworn testimony that the red stains were real Blood. Among the people there, one thought the Blood might have come from the priest's nose or mouth, but some surgeons who were present, after meticulous investigation, put these doubts to rest. Other clerical authorities intervened: the pro-vicar with the curia secretary and the vicar for the Inquisition, R. Bordino. The latter, at the request of all those present, wrote an account of the miracle.

Another important proof of the miracle's authenticity is furnished by a document which relates how Msgr. Filippo Artico, Bishop of Asti, in 1841 had the chalice and the consecrated Host examined by some physicists, who confirmed the origin of the red stains. The Pious Association of Milliavacca has jealously guarded the relics of the miracle: the chalice stained with Blood, the Host (which unfortunately has decomposed and is little more than a very thin sheet), the paten, the corporal, and the gold-plated silver chalice.

In 1412, the prior of the Basilica of St. Mary in Bagno di Romagna, Fr. Lazarus da Verona, while celebrating Holy Mass, was assailed by strong doubts about the Real Presence of Jesus in the Most Blessed Sacrament. He had just pronounced the words of consecration over the wine when it was transformed into living Blood and began to overflow from the chalice and spill onto the corporal. Fr. Lazarus, profoundly moved and repentant, confessed to those present both his unbelief and the amazing miracle the Lord had worked before his very eyes.

Panoramic view of Santa Maria in Bagno

At Bagno di Romagna, in the Basilica of St. Mary of the Assumption, the relic of the Eucharistic miracle of the "Holy Cloth Soaked in Blood" is preserved. The historian Fortunio thus describes the miracle in his noted work *Annales Camalduenses*: "It was the year 1412. The Camaldolese Abbey of Santa Maria in Bagno (then a priory) was governed by Fr. Lazarus, who was of Venetian origin. While he was celebrating the Divine Sacrifice, he mentally experienced, by diabolical influence, a strong doubt concerning the Real Presence of Jesus in the Most Blessed Sacrament; then he saw the Sacred Species of the wine overflow the chalice and drip onto the corporal in the form of living Blood, and thus the corporal became soaked. At the sight of such a profound event, his emotion and perturbation of mind were unspeakable. In tears, he turned to the bystanders, confessing his unbelief and relating the miracle which had just taken place before his eyes."

The monk Lazarus was later transferred to Bologna as chaplain of the Camaldolese nuns' Convent of St. Christine, where he died in 1416. The Camaldolese were in charge of the parish church in Bagno until the Napoleonic suppression of 1808; from

Picture in the basilica depicting the miracle

Relic of the Blood-stained corporal

Basilica of Santa Maria di Bagno di Romagno

Chapel with the urn of Bl. Giovanna

Detail of the Blood stains present on the corporal of the miracle

Interior of the basilica

then on the parish-Basilica of St. Mary of the Assumption, after having been held for a brief period by the diocese of Sansepolcro, in 1975 was definitively assigned to the diocese of Cesena.

In 1912, Cardinal Giulio Boschi, Archbishop of Ferrara, celebrated the fifth centenary of the miracle, which was followed by a Eucharistic studies conference. In 1958, His Excellency Domenico Bornigia had a chemical analysis done of the marks on the miraculous corporal at the University of Florence. The analysis confirmed that the stains were actually Blood.

In the basilica is found a colored and very unusual incision on wood from 1400 called "The Madonna of the Blood," which is found in the third chapel on the left. This image is thus named because, as Benedetto Tenaci, abbot of Bagno and eyewitness of the miracle on May 20, 1498, tells us, the icon bled from the left arm. Every year on the Feast of Corpus Christi, the corporal is carried in procession through the streets of the city. It is displayed every Sunday during the temperate season, which lasts from March to November, at the 11 AM Mass.

In 1263, a priest from Prague who was traveling in Italy was celebrating Mass in the basilica in Bolsena. When the moment of consecration arrived, a miracle took place: the Host was transformed into Flesh. This miracle strengthened the wavering belief of the priest in the Real Presence of Christ in the Eucharist. The Sacred Species were immediately inspected by Pope Urban IV and by St. Thomas Aquinas. This miracle helped convince the Pope to extend the feast of Corpus Christi to the universal Church "so that this excellent and venerable Sacrament might become for all a memorial of the extraordinary love God has for us."

*T*he Eucharistic miracle of Bolsena, depicted by Raphael in a well-known fresco in the Vatican Palace, took place in 1263. A German priest, Peter of Prague, stopped at Bolsena while on a pilgrimage to Rome. He was pious, but he found it difficult to accept that Christ was actually present in the consecrated Host. While celebrating Holy Mass above the tomb of St. Christina (located in the church named for this martyr), he spoke the words of consecration, and immediately Blood started to seep from the consecrated Host and trickle over his hands and onto the altar. At first the priest tried to hide the Blood, but eventually he interrupted the Mass and asked to be taken to the neighboring city of Orvieto, where Pope Urban IV resided.

The Pope sent emissaries to investigate. When the facts were ascertained, he ordered the Bishop of the diocese to bring the Host and the linen cloth bearing the stains of Blood to him. He had the relics placed in the cathedral. The linen bearing the spots of Blood is still reverently enshrined and exhibited in the Cathedral of Orvieto.

Cathedral of St. Christina in Bolsena

The Procession Over the Riochiaro Bridge (artist: Ugolino d'Ilario). Orvieto Cathedral

Flower petal pathways in honor of the miracle

Church of St. Christina in Bolsena, the altar where the miracle took place

Pope Urban IV was prompted by this miracle to commission St. Thomas Aquinas to compose the Office for the Mass and Liturgy of the Hours to celebrate the Most Holy Body of the Lord (Corpus Christi). One year after the miracle, in August of 1264, Pope Urban IV introduced Aquinas' composition, and, by means of a papal bull, instituted the feast of Corpus Christi.

The Eucharistic Miracle

"Suddenly the Host appeared in a visible way as true Flesh, sprinkled with red Blood..."

Tabernacle containing one of the Blood-stained stones of the miracle, Bolsena

Detail of the Blood-stained stone, Bolsena

Reliquary of the corporal. Ugolino d'Ilario's studio (1338), Orvieto

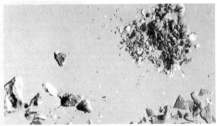

Fragments of the miraculous Host

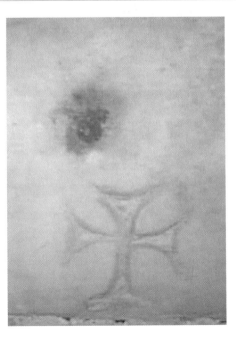

Painting by Francesco Trevisani

Painting of the Holy Mass of Bolsena by Francesco Robbio. From the collection of the Museum of the Diocese of Milan

Inside Orvieto's cathedral

John Paul II during his pastoral visit to Orvieto (June 17, 1990)

Detail of the reliquary

Orvieto Cathedral, Chapel of the Sacred Corporal

Detail of the *Mass of Bolsena*. Raphael (1513), Vatican Museums

Francesco Trevisani. *The Miracle of Bolsena,* detail

Parchment from the period of the miracle, notarized by Cesare Severo Durantino

Public adoration on the Feast of Corpus Christi, Orvieto

Fr. Antonio Reinardi's deep faith in the Eucharist was responsible for saving the village of Canosio from the torrential floods of the Maira River by means of a blessing with the Blessed Sacrament. There were many conversions among those who witnessed the miracle. To this day, during the octave of Corpus Christi the townspeople of Canosio celebrate a feast commemorating the miracle.

Parish church of Canosio

*C*anosio is a small village in the region of Val Maira, in the diocese of Saluzzo. In 1630, the townspeople had grown cold in their religious observance due to the spread of the Calvinist heresy.

The day after the feast of Corpus Christi, the Maira River flooded because of a torrential rainfall. The flood waters were so violent and powerful that some massive stones were dislodged from the mountainside and threatened to destroy the valley and the village itself. Fr. Antonio Reinardi, the pastor of the town, rang the church bells to assemble the people and exhorted them to pray that the Lord would stop the flood. He vowed that if the village of Canosio were spared from the flood's destruction, the townspeople would always celebrate an annual feast of Corpus Christi. Fr. Reinardi then placed the Blessed Sacrament in the monstrance. He processed towards the raging flood with some of the faithful as they all recited the *"Miserere"* Psalm 51. After he blessed the raging waters, the rain stopped at once and the flood waters immediately returned to their normal level. This incident revived the faith of the townspeople of Canosio, and

The Maira River

Panoramic view of Canosio

to this day they observe Fr. Reinardi's vow.

Unfortunately, many of the 17th-century documents preserved in the parish archives attesting to the miracle, were burned during the war between France and Spain. What is extant, however, is a copy of the document describing the events, left by the pastor who was an eyewitness.

In 1330, at Cascia, a gravely ill peasant had the priest called to bring him Communion. Instead of taking the pyx with him to carry the Eucharist to the sick man's house, the priest, partly through carelessness and partly through apathy, irreverently stuck a Host in a prayer book. When he reached the peasant's home, the priest opened the book and was filled with fear when he saw that the Host had been transformed into a clot of Blood which had stained the pages.

Relic of the Eucharistic miracle

*I*n Cascia, at the basilica dedicated to St. Rita which contains her body, there is also preserved a relic of a famous Eucharistic miracle which took place near Siena in 1330. A priest was asked to bring Communion to a sick peasant. The priest took a consecrated Host which he irreverently stuck in the pages of his breviary, and went to see the peasant. When he arrived at the house, after hearing the sick man's confession, the priest opened the book to take out the Host which he had placed there. To his great surprise he found that the Host was stained with living Blood, dampening both pages between which the Blessed Sacrament had been placed. The priest, confused and penitent, immediately went to Siena to the Augustinian Priory to ask counsel of Fr. Simone Fidati of Cascia, known by all to be a holy man. Fr. Fidati, having heard the story, pardoned the priest and asked to keep the two pages stained with Blood. Many Popes have promoted veneration of this miracle and granted indulgences.

In the 1687 act of recognition of the relic of the Eucharistic miracle of Cascia, a text was also cited from a very ancient code of the Priory of St.

Tabernacle of the Eucharistic miracle

Chapel where the relic is kept in the lower basilica

A man's face can clearly be seen

Priory of St. Augustine in Cascia

Enlarged reproduction of the face which appeared on the left-hand page

Enlarged reproduction of the face which appeared on the right-hand page

A man's face can clearly be seen

Urn containing the body of St. Rita which is preserved intact

Ancient monstrance which contained the relic of the miracle

Upper basilica with presbytery by the sculptor Manzu

The oldest depiction of St. Rita

Basilica of St. Rita

Augustine, which provides extensive information regarding the miracle. In addition to this source, the episode is also mentioned in the Communal Statutes of Cascia of 1387 where, among other things, it was ordained that "every year on the Feast of Corpus Christi, the authorities, the consuls, and all the people of Cascia should meet in the Church of St. Augustine and follow the clergy, who should carry the venerable relic of the Most Holy Body of Christ in procession through the city."

Painting depicting Bl. Simon Fidati

In 1930, on the sixth centenary of the event, a Eucharistic Congress was celebrated at Cascia for the entire diocese of Norcia. A precious and artistic monstrance was consecrated, and all the available historical documentation on the miracle was published.

The "Feast of Castello" has been faithfully celebrated since 1657. It recalls the May 25, 1656 liberation of the city of Cava from the plague on Ascension Thursday. The plague was ended by a procession and blessing with the Holy Eucharist which started from the hamlet of the Annunciation and proceeded to the higher terrace of Monte Castello.

*I*n May of 1656, a terrible epidemic of the plague overtook the city of Naples as a result of the invasion by Spanish troops from Sardinia. The plague spread so quickly to the neighboring villages and the surrounding countryside that it was soon at the gates of the city of Cava dei Tirreni. The victims numbered in the thousands, both in the villages and in the cities. Fr. Paolo Franco, one of the few who had been spared, was divinely inspired to brave all dangers and lead the people in a procession of reparation up to the summit of Mt. Castello. When they arrived at the top of the mountain, Fr. Franco blessed Cava dei Tirreni with the Blessed Sacrament. The plague miraculously ceased. To this day the townspeople commemorate the miracle in June with solemn annual processions.

Panoramic view of Cava dei Tirreni

An old print (ca. 18th century) depicting the miracle

The Eucharistic miracle is recalled each year during the *Sagra di Montecastello*

The annual fireworks at Cava on the anniversary of the miracle

The view from the mountain from which the priest blessed the city

In 1631, a young farm girl foolishly kindled a fire with dry hay. Because of high winds, the fire spread throughout a whole neighborhood in the town of Dronero. Every attempt to extinguish the flames proved useless. Only when a Capuchin friar, Fr. Maurice da Ceva, made the sign of the cross with the Blessed Sacrament did the fire miraculously die out.

The countryside around Dronero

Dronero

The chapel from which the Blessed Sacrament was taken. The stone tablet describes the miracle

On the afternoon of Sunday, August 3, 1631, towards the hour for Vespers, a great fire broke out in the commercial district of Saluzzo in the town of Dronero. A young farm girl had foolishly kindled a fire with dry hay at the same time as the wind was rising because of an approaching thunderstorm. The flames quickly and violently spread to the area of Borgo Maira. The townspeople desperately attempted to extinguish the fire, but all their efforts proved useless. Fr. Maurice da Ceva, a Capuchin, was inspired to have recourse to the power of the Lord in the Blessed Sacrament. He immediately organized a solemn procession with the Blessed Sacrament, followed by all the townspeople, to the location of the fire. The moment the Blessed Sacrament arrived, the flames miraculously died out! This miraculous event is described in detail on a stone tablet in the small Church of St. Brigid. On the Feast of Corpus Christi, the citizens of Dronero honor the memory of this miracle with a solemn annual procession of the Blessed Sacrament.

At San Mauro la Bruca, thieves broke into the church and stole several sacred objects; one was a ciborium containing consecrated Hosts. The Hosts were found the following morning. They are still intact today.

Interior of the church

The façade of the Church of San Mauro

The ostensorium where the miraculous Hosts are preserved

On the night of July 25, 1969, thieves broke into the parish church of San Mauro la Bruca with the intention of stealing some of the more precious objects. After they had pried open the tabernacle, they took a ciborium containing numerous consecrated Hosts. Once they left the church, the thieves emptied the ciborium and threw the Hosts onto a footpath. On the following morning a child noticed the pile of Hosts at an intersection and gathered Them up, immediately giving Them to the pastor. It was only in 1994, after 25 years of meticulous investigation, that Bishop Biagio D'Agostino of Vallo della Lucania acknowledged the

View of San Mauro la Bruca

miraculous preservation of the Hosts and authorized the cult of the miracle. Any chemical and scientific analysis shows that after just 6 months, normal unleavened wheat flour deteriorates significantly, and in a couple of years at the most, turns to mush and then, finally, to dust.

This Eucharistic miracle took place in Ferrara, in the Basilica of Santa Maria in Vado, on Easter Sunday, March 28, 1171. While breaking the consecrated Host during Easter Mass, Fr. Pietro da Verona, the basilica's prior, saw Blood gushing from It, sprinkling the vaulted ceiling above the altar with droplets. In 1595 the ceiling was enclosed within a small shrine and is still visible today in the monumental Basilica of Santa Maria in Vado.

Shrine that encloses the Holy Ceiling Vault (1594). Right side of the cross

On March 28, 1171, the prior of the Canons Regular Portuensi, Fr. Pietro da Verona, was celebrating Easter Mass with three confreres (Bono, Leonardo and Aimone). At the breaking of the consecrated Host, Blood gushed out of the Host and sprayed large drops on the ceiling above the altar. The stories tell of the "holy fear of the celebrant and of the immense wonder of the people who crowded the tiny church." There were many eyewitnesses who told of seeing the Host take on a bloody color and of having seen the figure of a Baby in the Host. Bishop Amato of Ferrara and Archbishop Gerard of Ravenna were immediately informed of the event.

They witnessed with their own eyes the miracle, namely "the Blood which we saw redden the ceiling." The church immediately became a pilgrimage destination, and was later rebuilt and enlarged on the orders of Duke Ercole I d'Este beginning in 1495.

There are many sources regarding this miracle. Among the most important is the bull of Pope Eugene IV (March 30, 1442), in which the pontiff mentions the miracle in reference to testimonies of the faithful and historical sources. The 1197 manuscript of Gerard Cambrense, conserved in Canterbury's Lambeth Library, is the oldest document which mentions the miracle. The miracle received recent attention in

John Paul II pauses before the ceiling vault in Ferrara

Bull of Eugene IV (1442)

Church of Santa Maria in Vado, Ferrara

Detail of the ceiling vault stained with Blood

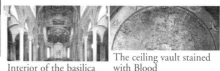
Interior of the basilica

The ceiling vault stained with Blood

the *Gemma Ecclesiastica* by historian Antonio Samaritani. Another document which dates back to March 6, 1404, is the bull of Cardinal Migliorati, in which he grants indulgences to "those who visit the church and adore the Miraculous Blood." Even today, on the 28th of every month in the basilica, which is currently under the care of Saint Gaspar del Bufalo's Missionaries of the Most Precious Blood, Eucharistic adoration is held in memory of the miracle. Every year, in preparation for the Feast of Corpus Christi, the solemn Forty Hours devotion is celebrated. The eighth centenary of the miracle was celebrated in 1971.

Bodini, *The Miracle of the Blood.* Painting on the ceiling near the shrine

The reliquaries of two Eucharistic miracles which took place in 1230 and 1595 are kept in Florence's St. Ambrose Church. In 1230, a distracted priest left several drops of the Precious Blood in the chalice after Mass. The next day, returning to celebrate Mass in the same church, he found in the chalice drops of living Blood, coagulated and turned into flesh. The Blood was immediately placed in a crystal cruet. The other Eucharistic miracle took place on Good Friday in 1595, when several consecrated Hosts were miraculously unharmed in a church fire.

1230 The first miracle took place on December 30, 1230. A priest named Fr. Uguccione, having finished celebrating Mass, did not realize that several drops of consecrated wine were still in the chalice and had turned into Blood. The historian Giovanni Villani gives a precise description of the miracle: "A day later, taking up the chalice, he found living Blood coagulated [...] and this was shown to all the nuns and locals who were present, to the bishop, and to all the clergy. Then the Precious Blood was shown to all the Florentines, who gathered around with great devotion to look. They took the Precious Blood from the chalice and put It in a crystal cruet which was again shown to the people with great reverence." Bishop Ardingo of Pavia ordered that the reliquary be brought to him. He kept the Precious Blood for several weeks before returning It to the sisters in the monastery for safekeeping in St. Ambrose Church. Pope Boniface IX, in 1399, granted the same indulgence as the Portiuncula to those faithful who visited St. Ambrose Church and contributed to adorning the reliquary of the miracle.

The 750th anniversary of the miracle was celebrated in 1980. The relic of the coagulated Blood (several drops of Blood which measure about half an inch square) is conserved in a reliquary which has been placed inside a white marble tabernacle constructed by Mimo da Fiesole.

Reliquary of the Hosts that survived the fire

Basilica of St. Ambrose, Florence

Fresco in the basilica depicting the first miracle that took place in 1230, showing the priest Uguccione carrying the Blood in procession

Reliquary of the drops of wine transformed into living Blood

1595 On Good Friday 1595, a lit candle on the altar in a side chapel called "The Sepulcher" fell to the ground and started a fire. The people immediately rushed to put out the fire and succeeded in saving the Blessed Sacrament and the chalice. In the great commotion, six consecrated Hosts fell from the pyx onto the burning carpet, but despite the fire They were found intact and joined together. In 1628, Archbishop Marzio Medici of Florence examined the Hosts, which he found to be incorrupt. He had the Sacred Species placed in a precious reliquary. Every May during the Forty Hours devotion, the two relics are exposed

Interior of the Basilica of St. Ambrose

Precious tabernacle, executed by Mino da Fiesole, where the relics of the two miracles are kept

Detail of the tabernacle where the relics of the two Eucharistic miracles are kept

together in a reliquary which also contains a consecrated Host for public adoration.

Among the most authoritative documents describing the Eucharistic miracle of Gruaro in 1294 is that of local historian Antonio Nicoletti (1765). In the public wash-house of Versiola, a woman was washing one of the altar linens from the Church of St. Justus. Suddenly she saw the altar linen become tinged with Blood. Observing more closely, she noted that the Blood was flowing from a consecrated Host remaining among the folds of the cloth.

The Blood-stained linen cloth is kept in the Church of the Most Holy Body of Christ in Valvasone

The relic of this miracle is kept in the Church of the Most Holy Body of Christ in Valvasone, but the miracle happened in Gruaro. In 1294, a young housemaid went to the public wash-house of Versiola to wash the altar linens from the Church of St. Justus in Gruaro. Suddenly, the woman noticed that a consecrated Host had been left by mistake among the folds of the cloth and that It was bleeding. Frightened by this inexplicable event, she immediately ran to alert the pastor, who then informed the Bishop of Concordia, Giacomo di Ottonello from Cividale. The Bishop, having learned the facts, wanted to keep the cloth in his cathedral in Concordia. However, the pastor of Gruaro and the counts of Valvasone, benefactors of the churches of Gruaro and of Valvasone, wanted to keep the cloth. No agreement was reached, so they had recourse to the Holy See. In the end, Rome let the counts keep the relic on condition that they would build a church dedicated to the Most Holy Body of Christ. The construction of the church was completed in 1483.

The oldest and most authoritative document describing the miracle is a decree of Pope Nicholas V written in 1454. The title of the parish church, formerly St. Mary and St. John the Evangelist, was thereby changed to the Church of the Most Holy Body of Christ (March 28, 1454). Today the cloth is kept in a crystal cylinder, held

Exact spot on the River Maira where the woman washed the cloth of the miracle

Detail of the corporal

Reliquary built by a Venetian craftsman in 1755

Maira Stream

Notarized copy of Pope Nicholas V's decree in 1454 permitting the counts of Valvasone to keep the relic of the miracle on condition that they build a shrine in honor of the Most Holy Body of Christ

Church of St. Justus in Gruaro

Interior of the Church of the Most Holy Body of Christ

Church of Gruaro. Rose window depicting the miracle

by a precious silver reliquary made by master craftsman Antonio Calligari. The celebration of the Holy Cloth is held on the fifth Thursday of Lent, at the end of several days of adoration of the Blessed Sacrament, with the participation of the priests and the community of Valvasone and the surrounding area. On the feast of Corpus Christi, the reliquary is carried in procession with the Most Blessed Sacrament.

Large memorial built to recall the miracle and the reconciliation between Gruaro and Valvasone

An inscription in marble from the 17th century describes this Eucharistic miracle which occurred in Lanciano in 750 at the Church of St. Francis. "A monastic priest doubted whether the Body of Our Lord was truly present in the consecrated Host. He celebrated Mass and, when he pronounced the words of consecration, he saw the Host turn into Flesh and the wine turn into Blood. All this was shown to those present. The Flesh is still intact and the Blood is divided into five unequal parts which together weigh the same *as each one* does separately."

Painting in the Valsecca Chapel depicting the miracle

*I*n 1970, the Archbishop of Lanciano and the Provincial Superior of the Conventual Franciscans in Abruzzo, with Rome's approval, asked Dr. Edward Linoli, director of the hospital in Arezzo and professor of anatomy, histology, chemistry, and clinical microscopy, to carry out a thorough scientific examination of the relics of the miracle which had occurred twelve centuries earlier. On March 4, 1971, the professor presented a detailed report of the various studies carried out. Here are the basic results:

1. The "miraculous Flesh" is authentic flesh consisting of muscular striated tissue of the myocardium.

2. The "miraculous Blood" is truly blood. The chromatographic analysis indicated this with absolute and indisputable certainty.

3. The immunological study shows with certitude that the flesh and the blood are human, and the immuno-hematological test allows us to affirm with complete objectivity and certitude that both belong to the same blood type, AB—the same blood type as that of the Man of the Shroud and the type most characteristic of Middle Eastern populations.

4. The proteins contained in the blood have the normal distribution, in the identical percentage as that of the serousproteic chart for normal fresh blood.

5. No histological dissection has revealed any trace of salt infiltrations or preserva-

Stone tablet from 1631 describing the miracle

Monstrance containing the sacred relics

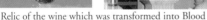

Relic of the wine which was transformed into Blood

tive substances used in antiquity for the purpose of embalming.

Professor Linoli also disproved the hypothesis of a hoax carried out in past centuries. This report was published in *The Sclavo Notebooks in Diagnostics* (Collection #3, 1971) and aroused great interest in the scientific world. Also, in 1973, the chief advisory board of the World Health Organization appointed a scientific commission to corroborate Linoli's findings. Their work lasted 15 months and included 500 tests. It was verified that the fragments taken from Lanciano could in no way be likened to mummified tissue. As to the nature of the fragment of flesh, the commission declared it to be living tissue because it responded rapidly to all the clinical reactions distinctive of living beings. The Flesh and the Blood of Lanciano are just that, flesh and blood, in the same condition one would expect to find flesh and blood taken the same day from a living human. Their reply fully corroborated Professor Linoli's conclusions. The extract summarizing the scientific work of the Medical Commission of the WHO and the UN, published in Dec. 1976 in New York and Geneva, declared that science, aware of its limits, has come to a halt, face to face with the impossibility of giving an explanation.

The Flesh and Blood of Lanciano are just as fresh as if they had been taken today from a living person.

Painting depicting the miracle

Il Sommo Pontefice Giovanni Paolo II allora Cardinale di Cracovia davanti alle Ss. Reliquie, cosi espresse la Sua devozione:

3. XI · 1979

Fac nos tibi semper magis credere in te spem habere, te diligere

+ Karol car. Wojtyla
arcivescovo di Cracovia

Card fom the visit of Cardinal Karol Wojtyla in 1979.

The 5 clots of Blood as seen with a magnifying glass. In the Blood of the miracle can be recognized all the components present in fresh blood, and the miracle within the miracle: each of the 5 clots of Blood weighs 15.85 grams, which is the identical weight of the 5 clots weighed together!

Cubical lattice in gold-plated cast iron in which the relics were preserved for almost 266 years, today returned to the Valsecca family chapel.

The 18th-century reliquary containing the Host and the coagulated Blood, the generous gift of Domenico Coli.

The Flesh consists of part of the myocardium, more precisely of the left ventricle. The arteries and veins can be easily identified, as well as a double, slender branch of the vagus nerve. At the time of the miracle, the Flesh was living and then submitted to the law of rigor mortis.

The miracle was the object of several official acknowledgements on the part of the ecclesiastical authorities between 1574 and 1886, not to mention

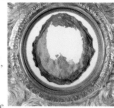

most recently, in 1970, when it was subjected to a scientific examination at the University of Siena, which concluded: "The flesh is true human flesh (formed by muscular tissue from the heart); the blood is true blood (belonging to the same blood type AB as the flesh); the component substances are those of human tissues, normal and fresh; the conservation of the flesh and the blood, left in their natural state for twelve centuries and exposed to the influence of atmospheric and biological elements, remains an extraordinary phenomenon" (*The Linoli Report* 4131971).

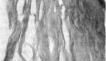

Histological view of the Flesh

The muscular fiber cells

A lobe of adipose tissue

A vagus nerve

St. Francis Church was built about 500 years later, in 1258, over the chapel where the miracle took place

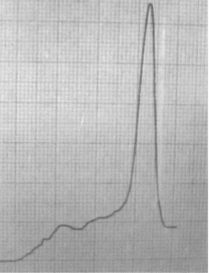

Graph of the electrophoresis of the proteins in the Blood of the miracle. The profile of the protein fractions from the serum could be superimposed on that of a standard specimen of fresh blood

On April 25, 1356, in Macerata, an unnamed priest was celebrating Mass in the chapel of St. Catherine's Church, owned by Benedictine nuns. During the breaking of the Eucharist before Holy Communion, the priest began to doubt the Real Presence of Jesus in the consecrated Host. At that moment, he was seized with great fear as he saw Blood beginning to flow from the Host, staining part of the corporal and the chalice on the altar.

*A*t Macerata in the Cathedral of Our Lady of the Assumption and St. Julian, under the altar of the Most Blessed Sacrament, one can see and venerate the relic of the "corporal marked by Blood." Also preserved in this church is the parchment from the time of the miracle on which the miracle is described. Furthermore, the historian Ferdinando Ughelli cited this miracle in his 1647 work, *Italia Sacra,* and described how, since the fourteenth century, "the corporal has been carried in solemn procession through the city, enclosed in an urn of crystal and silver, with the concourse of all Piceno." All the documents are in agreement in their descriptions of how the miracle took place. An unnamed priest, during the Mass, was struck with strong doubts about the reality of transubstantiation, and when he broke the large Host, he saw Blood dripping from the Host and falling onto the corporal and chalice. The priest immediately informed Bishop Nicholas of San Martino, who ordered that the relic of the Blood-stained cloth be brought to the cathedral, and later instituted a regular canonical process.

In 1494, one of the first confraternities in honor of the Most Blessed Sacrament was instituted at Macerata, and it was here that the pious practice of the Forty Hours was established in 1556. Every year on the feast of Corpus Christi, the miraculous corporal is carried in procession behind the Most Blessed Sacrament.

Small parchment from 1356 on which is written: "Here came the flow of Blood of Our Lord Jesus Christ from the chalice on April 25 in the Year of Our Lord 1356"

Macerata's cathedral

View of Macerata

Chapel of the Most Blessed Sacrament where the relic is kept

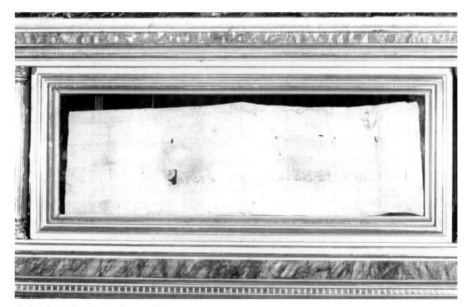

Relic of the Blood-stained corporal

In April 1604, a Eucharistic miracle took place in Mogoro. The event was described by historian Pietro M. Cossu. During Mass, two men in mortal sin dropped two Hosts onto the ground, leaving imprints of the Hosts on the stone floor. To commemorate this event and in reparation for the sacrilege, there is a solemn Eucharistic procession every year in Mogoro on the Sunday after Easter.

*I*n Mogoro on the Italian island of Sardinia, on the Monday after Easter in 1604, Fr. Salvatore Spiga, pastor of St. Bernard's Church, was celebrating Mass. After the Consecration he began distributing Holy Communion to the faithful. At a certain point, he saw in the Communion line two men who were well-known for the dissolute lives they led. The pastor gave them Holy Communion, but as soon as they had taken the Hosts into their mouths, they spat Them out onto the stone floor below the altar rail. The two men justified themselves by saying that the Hosts had become as hot as burning embers and that the Blessed Sacrament was burning their tongues. Then, taken by remorse at not first having gone to Confession, they ran away. Fr. Salvatore went to pick up the Hosts and saw that the imprints remained in the stone as if they had been carved there. He ordered the stone to be thoroughly washed in the hope that the imprints would be erased. But every attempt to eradicate the marks failed. Many historians, including Fr. Pietro Cossu and Fr. Casu, described the findings made by the Bishop at that time, Msgr. Antonio Surredo, and by his successors.

Eucharistic Miracle of Mogoro, Francesco Pinna (1604 – 1607).

Imprint of the first Host   Imprint of the second Host

Decorative case containing the stone of the miracle, Parish of St. Bernard

Parish of St. Bernard, Mogoro

Panoramic view of Mogoro

Among the most important documents confirming the miracle is a public act written by the notary Pedro Antonio Escano on May 25, 1686, in which the rector of Mogoro stipulates a contract for the construction of a gilded wooden tabernacle over the main altar. At the base of the tabernacle, there was to be an opening for the "stone of the miracle," which was to be enclosed in a decorative case and placed in such a way that the faithful could see it. The stone bears the imprint of the Hosts to this day.

In 1560 at Morrovalle, a huge fire completely destroyed a Franciscan church, but spared a large Host contained in a pyx (which was also completely burned except for the lid). The Eucharistic miracle's fourth centenary was solemnly celebrated in 1960, and the city council unanimously agreed to place over Morrovalle's main gate the inscription, *Civitas Eucaristica* (Eucharistic City).

*I*n Morrovalle, at about two o'clock on the morning of April 17, 1560, during the octave of Easter, the lay brother Angelo Blasi awoke with a start at the sound of violent crackling. Looking out the window of his cell, he saw that the church was completely engulfed in flames. He immediately ran to notify the other brothers. The fire was extinguished after seven hours.

During the following days, the work of clearing the massive pile of church ruins began. On April 27, Fr. Battista da Ascoli was removing a piece of marble from what used to be the main altar and discovered the pyx in a wall cav-

ity. Its corporal was scorched, but the consecrated Host was still intact and in perfect condition. Father Battista shouted at the sight of the miracle, and many people immediately ran to see the marvelous sight. For three entire days, the Blessed Sacrament was exposed for public adoration. When Franciscan Provincial Father Evangelista da Morro d'Alba finally arrived, the miraculous Host was placed in an ivory case.

The then-bishop of Bertinoro, Bishop Louis di Forli, was immediately sent by Pope Pius IV to Morrovalle to investigate the authenticity of the event. As soon as he received the Bishop's

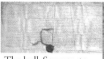

The bull *Sacrosancta Romana Ecclesia* of Pope Pius IV (1560), confirming the miracle

Morrovalle procession in honor of the miracle

Convent annexed to the Church of St. Francis where the miracle took place

Church of St. Bartholomew

Reliquary of the miracle

account, Pope Pius IV judged the occurrence to be unexplainable by natural causes, and he authorized public devotion with the bull *Sacrosancta Romana Ecclesia* (1560). The bull proclaims the anniversaries of the fire and the discovery of the Host (April 17 and 27) as feasts with plenary indulgences (so that they were known locally as the feasts "of the two pardons").

Because of the many faithful who came to the celebrations, the church was later expanded. Today, the feasts are celebrated with exposition of the Blessed Sacrament and of the reliquary on the main altar. The pardons, namely the plenary indulgences, can be gained at St. Bartholomew's Church. The miraculous Host was conserved intact until 1600, but due to the vicissitudes of history, every trace of this Host was later lost. All that remain today are the reliquary and the pyx lid which survived the flames.

The relics of a Eucharistic miracle which took place in 1273, in which the Host turned into bleeding Flesh, are kept in Offida at St. Augustine's Church. There are many documents describing this miracle, among which is an authentic copy of a parchment from the 13th century, written by the notary Giovanni Battista Doria in 1788. There are also many official bulls of the Popes, from that of Boniface VIII (1295) to that of Sixtus V (1585), as well as discourses of Roman congregations, episcopal decrees, communal statutes, votive gifts, memorial stones, frescoes and testimonies of notable historical figures, among whom we recall Antinori and Fella.

Frescoes in the church illustrating the miracle

In 1273 in the town of Lanciano, a woman named Ricciarella went to a witch to ask how she could regain the affection of her husband, Giacomo Stasio. Following the witch's advice, she went to Communion to obtain a consecrated Host. On her return home, she put the Host on the fire in an earthenware jar with the intention of turning the Blessed Sacrament into powder to put into her husband's food. The Host, however, was transformed into living Flesh. Ricciarella, terrified, wrapped the jar and the bloodied Host in a linen tablecloth which she then buried under the manure in her husband's stable. Strange events began to take place in the stable: every time Giacomo's donkey entered, it would genuflect toward the place where the miraculous Host was buried. Giacomo began to think that his wife had put a curse on the beast.

Seven years later, Ricciarella, tormented by remorse, confessed her terrible sacrilege to the prior of the Augustinian priory in Lanciano, Giacomo Diotallevi, a native of Offida. According to the oldest stories, the woman, in tears, began screaming, "I killed God! I killed God!" The priest went to the place and found the bundle of relics intact. These were later given to his fellow townsmen of Offida.

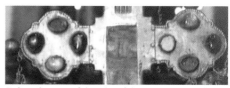

Detail of the Blood-stained linen

Earthenware jar in which the miracle took place, Offida

Relic of the linen with Blood spots where Richiarella enfolded the miraculous Host

Enlarged image of the relic of the Host contained in a precious cross made by a Venetian craftsman (13th century)

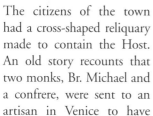

The citizens of the town had a cross-shaped reliquary made to contain the Host. An old story recounts that two monks, Br. Michael and a confrere, were sent to an artisan in Venice to have the reliquary made. When they arrived, they made the craftsman swear "that he would not reveal to anyone what he was about to see and place inside the cross. Having taken the oath, the craftsman reached out to take the pyx containing the miraculous Host, but, struck by a sudden fever, exclaimed, 'What have you brought me, O my brother?' The religious then asked him if he were in mortal sin. The craftsman answered in the affirmative. He made his confession to the same priest and, the fever having left him, he then took the pyx without any danger. Extracting the Host, he fixed both the Host and some wood from the True Cross inside the cross-shaped reliquary, with a crystal above it, as you can clearly see."

Relics of the miracle

The reliquaries of the jar and the Blood-stained linen with the cross containing the miraculous Host are exposed in St. Augustine's Church in Offida. Ricciarella's house in Lanciano was made into a small chapel. In 1973 the seventh centennial of the miracle was celebrated, and every year on May 3rd, the citizens of Offida celebrate the anniversary of the miracle.

The Eucharistic Miracle of
PATIERNO (NAPLES)
ITALY, 1772

On August 29, 1774, the Archbishop's curia rendered a favorable opinion regarding the miraculous finding and unexplainable preservation of the Hosts stolen from St. Peter's Church in Patierno on February 24, 1772. In 1971, a diocesan Eucharistic Year was proclaimed to remind the community of the Eucharistic miracle. Unfortunately, in 1978 some unknown thieves managed to steal the relic with the miraculous Hosts of 1772.

An old depiction of the miracle

In 1772, unknown thieves stole some consecrated Hosts which were found a month later on the lands of the Duke of Grottolelle underneath a pile of manure. However, the Hosts were completely intact. The appearance of mysterious lights and a dove led to the finding of the Hosts. St. Alphonsus Liguori described this miracle in detail and took the opportunity to reawaken the faith and devotion of the people towards the Eucharist.

The circumference of the Hosts stolen from St. Peter's Church in Patierno corresponded perfectly with the iron used to bake them, which was the property of that particular church. The vicar general, Msgr. Onorati, drew up the minutes of the diocesan process, which lasted two years, from 1772 to 1774. Msgr. Onorati also sealed with red Spanish wax the knot in the ribbon which tied shut the "two glass jars capped with silver." The minutes state, "We pronounce, decree and declare that the aforementioned lights and the intact preservation of the consecrated Hosts, which were underground for many days, was and is an authentic miracle worked by God to illustrate more and more the truth of Catholic dogma and increase worship towards the Real Presence of Christ in the Blessed Sacrament of the Eucharist."

Reliquary of the
miracle

St. Peter's Church,
Patierno

QUÍ
A PIÈ DI UN LETAMAIO
NEL XXVIII. GENNAIO
MDCCLXXII

A plaque at the place where the Hosts were found

Document in which Cardinal Ursi elevates St. Peter's
Church to a diocesan Eucharistic shrine

Among the various testimonies, there were also those of three renowned scientists of the time, among whom was Dr. Domenico Cotugno of the Royal University of Naples. They all agreed in saying that "emphatically, the extraordinary apparition of the lights in many varied ways, and the intact preservation of the unearthed Hosts cannot be explained by physical principles, and they surpass the power of natural agents. Therefore, they must be considered miraculous."

In 1972 Professor Pietro De Franciscis, professor of human physiology at the University of Naples, confirmed the above statement in his account, *Relazione sul ritrovamento delle sacre Ostie, avvenuto il 24 febbraio del 1772, in San Pietro a Patierno.*

In 1967, Cardinal Corrado Ursi, on the occasion of the elevation of St. Peter's Church to a diocesan Eucharistic shrine, said, "The prodigious event of St. Peter's in Patierno is a gift and a divine warning for the whole archdiocese. Its voice must never weaken but must urge the faithful of all times to consider the message regarding the 'Bread of Life for the salvation of the world' spoken of by Christ at Capharnaum."

This Eucharistic miracle was performed directly by St. Anthony after he was challenged by a certain Albigensian heretic named Bonovillo to demonstrate the truth of the Real Presence of Jesus in the Eucharist. The oldest biography of St. Anthony, *L'Assidua* (The Untiring), carries Bonovillo's exact words: "Friar! I tell you before all these people: I will believe in the Eucharist if my mule, after three days with no food, adores the Host which you offer him rather than eating the fodder I give him." The mule, despite the fact that it was exhausted by hunger, knelt before the Host and refused its food.

Miracle of Saint Anthony, collection of the Diocesan Museum of Milan

*I*n Rimini, it is still possible today to visit the church built in honor of the Eucharistic miracle performed by St. Anthony of Padua in 1227. This episode is also cited in *Begninitas*, considered one of the oldest sources regarding the life of St. Anthony. "This saintly man was debating with a faithless heretic who was opposed to the sacrament of the Eucharist and whom the saint had nearly led to the Catholic faith. But, after numerous arguments, this heretic declared: 'If you, Anthony, produce a miracle and demonstrate to me that Communion is truly the Body of Christ, I will completely renounce my heresy and immediately convert to the Catholic faith. Let's make a bet. I'll keep one of my beasts locked up for three days to feel the torments of hunger. Then I'll bring it forth in public and show it food. You will stand in front of it with what you maintain is the Body of Christ. If the beast, leaving aside its food, hurries to adore its God, I will share the faith of your Church.'" St. Anthony, illuminated and inspired from above, accepted the challenge.

At the chosen day and hour, the priest and the heretic entered the Grand Piazza (today the Three Martyrs Piazza) at the appointed hour. A huge crowd of curious people assembled as well. The

Altar constructed on the trunk of the column from which St. Anthony performed the miracle

Donatello di Niccolo di Betto Bardi, called Donatello. *Miracle of the Mule*, (1446-1448) Padua, Basilica of St. Anthony

Domenico Beccafumi, *St. Anthony and the Miracle of the Mule* (1537), Louvre, Paris

Eucharistic Miracle of St. Anthony, Salvaterra de Magos, Church Matriz, Portugal

Temple of the Most Holy Eucharist, Rimini

Fresco of Girolamo Tessari (1511). Basilica of St. Anthony, Padua

Church of St. Anthony, Tonara

protagonists of the unusual challenge were followed by their own sympathizers: St. Anthony was followed by Catholic faithful; Bonovillo (this was the name of the Albigensian heretic) by his allies in unbelief.

The saint held in his hands a monstrance containing the consecrated Host; the heretic held his starving mule. The saint, after having requested and obtained silence, turned to the mule with these words: "In the name of your Creator, Whom I, unworthy as I am, hold in my hands, I order you: Come forward immediately and render homage to the Lord with all due respect so that heretics and evildoers will understand that all creatures must humble themselves before their Creator whom priests hold in their hands at the altar." Immediately the animal, refusing the food offered by its master, docilely approached the priest. It bent its front legs before the Host and paused there reverently.

Anthony's adversary was true to his word and threw himself at the saint's feet, publicly renouncing the error of his ways. From that day on, he became one of the miracle-working saint's most zealous cooperators.

This Eucharistic miracle, the relic of which is still preserved at the Benedictine monastery in Andechs, Germany, took place in Rome in 595 during a Eucharistic celebration at which Pope St. Gregory the Great was presiding. At the moment of receiving Holy Communion, a Roman noblewoman began to laugh because she had doubts about the Real Presence of Christ in the consecrated Bread and Wine. The Pope, troubled by her disbelief, decided not to give her Communion, and suddenly the Bread turned into Flesh and Blood.

Adrien Ysenbrandt, 16th century. The apparition of Jesus with the signs of the Passion during the Mass of St. Gregory

*A*mong the most important works in which this Eucharistic miracle, which occurred in Rome in 595, is mentioned, is the *Vita Beati Gregorii Papae,* written by Deacon Paul in 787. It was customary in those times to have the Communion bread prepared by the parishioners themselves. Pope St. Gregory the Great was a direct eyewitness to this prodigy. One Sunday, while celebrating Mass in an ancient church dedicated to St. Peter, the Pope was distributing Communion and saw among the faithful in line, one of the women who had prepared the bread for the Consecration, and she was laughing out loud. Troubled, the Pope stopped her and asked her to explain her behavior. She excused herself by saying that she could not believe that the bread she had made with her very own hands could become the Body and Blood of Christ during the Consecration. St. Gregory denied her Communion and began to beg God to enlighten her. Having just finished praying, he saw that the very part of the bread prepared by the woman had become Flesh and Blood. The woman repented, knelt on the ground, and began to weep. To this day, part of the relic of the miracle is housed in Andechs, Germany, in the local Benedictine monastery.

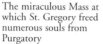

Mass of St. Gregory.
Museum Hiéron, Paray-
le-Monial

Church of the Benedictine
monastery in Andechs

The miraculous Mass at
which St. Gregory freed
numerous souls from
Purgatory

The chapel in Andechs
that houses the shrine

Old missal in which
St. Gregory is depicted
celebrating the Mass

The Miraculous Mass of St. Gregory the Great by
Domenico Cresti (1559 – 1638)

The shrine containing the Host of the miracle which
is preserved to this day in Andechs

The Eucharistic Miracle

Having just finished praying, he saw the very part of the bread prepared by the woman become Flesh and Blood.

Nicolò Circignani called the Pornarancio, *The Eucharistic Miracle of St. Gregory the Great*. The lunette of the portico in the entrance of the Church of San Gregorio Magno al Cielo, Rome

Church of San Gregorio Magno al Cielo, Rome

Icon of St. Gregory

One can still see today the miraculous imprint left by the Host which fell on the altar step in the Caetani Chapel of St. Pudentiana Church in Rome. The imprint on the step was left after the Host fell from the hands of a priest who, while celebrating Mass, was seized by doubts about the Real Presence of Christ in the Sacrament of the Eucharist.

Interior of the church

St. Pudentiana is one of the oldest churches in Rome. According to a great number of historians, the Roman Senator Pudente offered hospitality to the Apostle Peter in his home, which stood on the exact spot where the church's foundation now lies. The name of the church is that of the senator's daughter, Pudentiana.

Pudentiana and her sister Praxedes, although never martyred, became famous because they wiped up the blood of the martyrs after the latter were executed. The church is adorned with numerous Roman mosaics from the early Christian era and was constructed under Pope Pius I in 145 A.D. on the site where Senator Pudente's home had once stood, according to the wishes of his daughters Praxedes and Pudentiana. On the altar steps of the Caetani Chapel, constructed by the Caetani family, there is to this day an imprint and a stain of Blood left by a Host which fell from the hands of a priest as he was celebrating Mass. The priest had been overtaken by doubts about the Real Presence of Jesus in the consecrated Host, and immediately after the Consecration, he inadvertently dropped the Host to the ground, where the imprinted mark is still visible today.

St. Pudentiana Church, Rome

Steps in the chapel that clearly show the imprint of the fallen Host and the stain of Blood

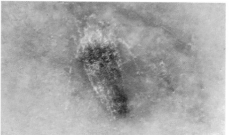

Detail of the stain of Blood left by the fallen Host

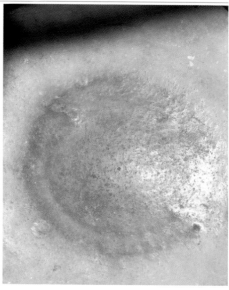

Detail of the impression left by the Host that fell onto the marble floor

ROSANO

In the monastery church in Rosano is venerated a statue of the Sacred Heart which bled and wept on various occasions. The statue, which is life-size, was donated in 1948 by a devout person to fulfill a promise made during World War II. Christ's face has an intense expression of manly sweetness which invites all to prayer and recollection. The Heart is in the center of His chest, surrounded by a crown of thorns.

Statue of the Sacred Heart that bled and wept

From Bishop Luciano Giovanotti's letter of April 4, 1998:

"On the evening of April 4, 1948, the first Sunday after Easter, during the chanting of Vespers, people noticed for the first time that tear-like drops were falling from the eyes of the statue. In June of that year, another stunning and unexpected miracle occurred – a flow of blood. These events occurred repeatedly between 1948 and 1950 and were corroborated by many eye-witnesses, by the nuns themselves and particularly by the abbess, Mother Ildegarde Cabitza of holy memory. In the monastery archives are preserved many sworn testimonies from priests, preachers and visitors, together with medical analyses of the blood and finger towels and purificators soaked

with blood. One of the most precious testimonies is that of Monsignor Angelo Scapecchi, who later became Auxiliary Bishop of the diocese of Arezzo. From the archives we learn of the investigation of the Visitator, Father Luigi Romoli, O.P., sent by the Holy Office, who personally interrogated all the nuns, imposing the strictest secrecy on the community. Subsequently, on November 14, 1950, the Holy Office ordered that the statue be removed so as to keep it in a secret location. It was brought back to Rosano in 1952.

"The community of nuns in Rosano experienced these events with intimate joy and great devotion but also with great discretion, so much so that, as we learn from the chronicles, they were not distracted

According to a 17th century inscription on the façade of the church, the Abbey of Santa Maria of Rosano was founded in 780

Entrance to the Abbey of Santa Maria of Rosano

Cloister

Abbey refectory

from their daily duties. On the contrary, they lived their monastic life even more intensely according to the Benedictine motto: *Ora et labora*. The weeping and the flow of blood were considered inexplicable from a natural and human point of view. My venerable predecessor, Bishop Giovanni Giorgis, saw in these events of Rosano an appeal from the Lord 'to fidelity, reparation and prayer.' [...] Beloved brothers and sisters, with softened hearts let us look back on the events that took place in our diocese fifty years ago and see them as signs of the Lord's benevolence and love and an invitation to serious and profound reflection. With great joy let us renew our ardent devotion to the Sacred Heart of Jesus. And as we receive this

The crypt

message, let us ask for the gift of an ever deeper conversion to His love, for the grace of an increase in apostolic fervor, and for the gift of numerous holy vocations to the priesthood and religious life, so as to make Christ the Heart of the world. Looking to the Heart of Jesus, we will draw water joyfully from the springs of salvation!"

A sorceress asked a woman to bring her a consecrated Host. The woman went to Mass, and during Communion she managed to hide a Host in her handkerchief. The priest noticed what she was doing and ran after her, ordering her to show him what she was hiding. The woman opened the handkerchief, and to the surprise of both, they saw that half of the stolen Particle had been transformed into Flesh and the other half looked like the Host.

St. Peter Damian

Hermitage of Fonte Avellana, where St. Peter Damian lived

*I*n his *Opuscul.* XXXIV; *Patrol. Lat.,* tom. CXLV, col. 573, St. Peter Damian, a Doctor of the Church, describes an important Eucharistic miracle of which he was a direct witness. We present the episode as the Saint himself describes it: "This is a Eucharistic event of great importance. It took place in 1050. Giving in to a horrible suggestion, a woman was about to take the Eucharistic Bread home to use the Sacred Species for sorcery. But a priest noticed what she had done and ran after her, taking back the Host she had sacrilegiously stolen. Then he unfolded the white linen cloth in which the Host had been wrapped and found that the Host had been transformed in such a way that half had visibly become the Body of Christ, while the other half preserved the normal look of a Host. By such a clear testimony, God wanted to win over unbelievers and heretics who refused to accept the Real Presence of the Eucharistic mystery: in one half of the consecrated Bread the Body of Christ was visible, while in the other half, the natural form remained, thus highlighting the reality of the sacramental transubstantiation which takes place at the Consecration."

In 1732, for more than three consecutive months, there appeared signs of Our Lord's Passion in the consecrated Hosts. This marvelous event took place during exposition of the Blessed Sacrament in the Monastery of the Most Holy Redeemer in Scala in the presence of numerous witnesses, among whom was St. Alphonsus Maria Liguori, the great Doctor of the Church.

Venerable Maria Celeste Crostarossa

Interior of the monastery church

Monstrance of the miracle

Monastery of the Most Holy Redeemer, Scala

*T*he venerable Sr. Maria Celeste Crostarosa founded the Monastery of the Most Holy Redeemer together with St. Alphonsus Maria Liguori. Every Thursday the Most Blessed Sacrament was exposed in the monastery for public adoration. From September 11, 1732, for three consecutive months, during solemn exposition of the Blessed Sacrament, signs of the Passion of Christ appeared in the Host contained in the monstrance. All this was confirmed not only by the nuns and the people but also by Bishop Santoro of Scala and by the Bishop of Castellamare. The apparition also occurred in the presence of St. Alphonsus Maria Liguori. Bishop Santoro wrote a letter to Bishop Simonetti, apostolic nuncio to Naples, in which he described all the details of the visions that took place in the Host which had been exposed. In turn, the nuncio forwarded the letter to Cardinal Barbieri, then secretary of state.

In the Basilica of St. Francis in Siena, 223 *consecrated Hosts* have remained intact for over 270 years. Archbishop Tiberio Borghese had some *unconsecrated* hosts sealed in a tin box for ten years. When the box was reopened, the scientific commission found only worms and rotted fragments. The Sienese event defies every physical and biological law. The scientist Enrico Medi stated: "This direct intervention from God is the miracle [...], accomplished and maintained for centuries, testifying to the permanent reality of Christ in the Sacrament of the Eucharist."

The Sacred Hosts in the processional monstrance

*A*mong the most important documents describing this miracle is a memoir written by a certain Macchi in 1730. He records that on August 14, 1730, thieves stole a ciborium containing 351 consecrated Hosts from the Basilica of St. Francis in Siena. Three days later, on August 17th, the 351 consecrated Hosts were found intact in the dust of the alms box in the sanctuary of Santa Maria in Provenzano. The entire population celebrated the finding of the consecrated Hosts, which were immediately taken to the Basilica of St. Francis in solemn procession.

The Hosts have not changed in appearance with the passage of time. Distinguished men have examined them numerous times by every means available, and the conclusion has always been the same: "The Sacred Hosts are still fresh, intact, physically uncorrupted, and chemically pure, showing no sign of any principle of corruption." In 1914, Pope St. Pius X authorized an examination carried out by numerous nutritionists, health specialists, chemists and pharmacists, among whom was the well-known Professor Siro Grimaldi.

The final conclusion stated: "The Hosts of Siena are a classic example of the perfect conservation of particles of unleavened bread, consecrated in the year 1730, and constitute a singular

This painting by Master Stefano di Giovanni, known as "il Sassetta," is preserved in England in the Bowes Museum in Barnard Castle. It depicts the scene of another Eucharistic miracle that took place near Siena in a Carmelite monastery. A Carmelite monk, tormented by doubts regarding the Real Presence of Jesus in the Blessed Sacrament, is freed from the devil after receiving Communion.

Basilica of St. Francis, Siena

Interior of the basilica

His Holiness John Paul II in 1980 in Siena in adoration before the Hosts of the miracle

The Sacred Hosts of Siena

Detail of a painting depicting the Hosts of the miracle in Santa Maria in Provenzano

phenomenon which reverses the natural laws of conservation of organic matter… It is strange, surprising, abnormal… The laws of nature have been reversed. The glass had mold on it, but the unleavened bread was more resistant [to mold] than crystal [...] This is a unique fact in the annals of science." Additional tests were done in 1922 (when the Hosts were transferred into a cylinder of pure crystal), and also in 1950 and 1951. Pope John Paul II, during a pastoral visit to Siena on September 14, 1980, said in the presence of the miraculous Hosts: "It is the Real Presence!"

The permanent miracle of the Sacred Hosts is kept in the Piccolimini Chapel

Fourteen tests were carried out to ascertain the condition of the Hosts. The most scientific one was the one requested by St. Pius X in 1914, carried out in the presence of many scientists.

in the summer months and, in winter, in the Martinozzi Chapel. Numerous events show the honor in which the Sienese hold the Sacred Hosts, such as the solemn Corpus Christi procession, the Eucharistic ceremony at the end of September, and the day of Eucharistic adoration on the 17th of each month.

A non-Christian woman, who did not believe in the Catholic dogma of the Real Presence of Jesus in the Eucharist, managed with the help of a Christian friend to steal a consecrated Host during a Mass. The woman, as if she were challenging God, put the consecrated Host into a pan of boiling oil. Suddenly the Host spilled out masses of Blood, which poured onto the floor and out the door of the house.

A representation of the miracle

To this day in Trani, in the region of Puglia, the relic of this Eucharistic miracle, which took place around the year 1000, is housed in the Cathedral of St. Mary of the Assumption. Numerous documents retell the miracle; among them are Eucharistic monograms reproduced on the ancient streets of the city. The friar Bartolomeo Campi, in his work *L'Inamorato di Gesù Cristo* (1625), gives us an accurate account of the facts: "Pretending to be Christian, the woman received Communion with the others… and took the consecrated Host from her mouth and put It in a handkerchief. Once home, she wanted to see whether or not the Blessed Sacrament was bread, so she put the consecrated Host in a heated pan filled with oil, to fry It. Upon contact with

the boiling oil, the consecrated Host miraculously turned into bloody Flesh, and a hemorrhage, so to speak, would not stop flowing, spilling from the pan all over the cursed woman and her house. Terrified, the woman began to scream… and the neighbors immediately ran to find out the reason for her cries…."

The Archbishop was immediately informed of the events, and he ordered that the consecrated Host be reverently returned to the church. The Cistercian Abbot Ferdinando Ughelli (1670), in his well-known encyclopedic work *Italia Sacra,* wrote in the seventh volume: "In Trani is venerated a sacred Host which was fried out of hatred of our Faith …; the true Flesh and

Padre Pio said: "Trani is fortunate because its land has been bathed twice in the Blood of Christ."

The pan the woman used to fry the Host

Interior of the sacrilegious woman's house, converted into a chapel in 1706

St. Andrew's Church where the host was retrieved from the sacrilegious woman

House where the miracle took place, which has since been converted into a chapel

Chapel dedicated to the miracle where the precious reliquary is housed, St. Andrew's Church

Reliquary containing the miraculous Host from the 17th century

Blood of Christ were unveiled in the unleavened Bread which fell to the ground." An indirect confirmation of this miracle is also found in a remark of St. Padre Pio of Pietrelcina, who exclaimed: "Trani is fortunate to have been bathed by the Blood of Christ twice," the first reference being to this miracle and the second to the miracle of the Colonna Crucifix from which an abundant stream of Blood flowed from Jesus' nose. Thanks to the generosity of the nobleman Ottaviano Campitelli, the woman's house was converted into a chapel in 1706.

Detail of the painting by Paolo Uccello depicting the miracle. Museum of Urbino

In 1616 the Host was transferred to an antique silver shrine donated by Fabrizio de Cunio. Throughout the years, many tests have been performed on this sacred relic, the last one in 1924 at the Interdiocesan Eucharistic Congress headed by Msgr. Giuseppe Maria Leo.

Interior of Trani's cathedral

Cathedral of Holy Mary of the Assumption in Trani. For many years the relics of the miracle were kept here.

Inside the Corpus Domini Basilica in Turin, there is an iron railing enclosing the place where, in 1453, the first Eucharistic miracle of Turin occured. An inscription inside the railing describes the miracle: "Here the she-mule carrying the Divine Body fell prostrate; here the Sacred Host was miraculously freed from the bag containing It and rose on high; here It came gently down among the suppliant hands of the people of Turin; here then, is the place made holy by the miracle. Remembering, pray on your knees. (June 6, 1453)"

On entering the Basilica of Corpus Domini in Turin, one immediately notices over the altar a painting by Bartolomeo Garavaglia, a student of Guercino. It portrays the great Eucharistic miracle of 1453.

*I*n the Alta Val Susa, close to Exilles, the army of René D'Angiò met the army of Duke Ludwig of Savoy. The soldiers plundered the town. Some of them went to the church, and one of them, forcing open the tabernacle's small door, stole the monstrance with the consecrated Host. He wrapped it up in a bag and headed for Turin by mule.

In Turin, in the main square close to St. Sylvester's Church (now Holy Spirit Church, where later the Church of Corpus Domini was built), his mule stumbled and fell. Suddenly the bag fell open and, to the great wonder of the bystanders, the monstrance with the consecrated Host rose into the air over the surrounding houses. Among those present was Fr. Bartholomew Coccolo. He ran with this news to Bishop Ludwig. The Bishop, accompanied by a group of people and clergy, went to the plaza, prostrated himself in adoration, and prayed with the words of the Emmaus disciples, *"Stay with us, Lord."* Meanwhile a new miracle occurred; the monstrance had fallen to the ground, leaving the consecrated Host free and shining like the sun. The Bishop, who was holding a chalice, lifted it up high, and the consecrated Host slowly began to descend and settled into the chalice.

Devotion to the miracle of 1453 took root immediately in Turin. The city first built a chapel on the spot of the miracle. This was soon replaced by the church

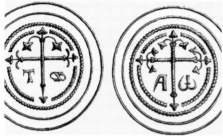

Imprints of the miraculous Host

Commemorative plaque, Turin

Depictions of the miracle of Turin

Basilica of Corpus Domini, Turin

dedicated to the Corpus Domini. But the most significant display of this devotion is expressed by the celebrations organized on the centenaries and fiftieth anniversaries (1653, 1703, 1853, and 1803).

The documents recounting the miracle are many. The oldest are the three Capitulary Acts of 1454, 1455 and 1456, and some contemporary writings of the city of Turin. In 1853 Blessed Pope Pius IX solemnly celebrated the fourth centenary of the miracle. St. John Bosco and Fr. Rua participated in this celebration. Furthermore, Pius IX on this occasion approved the Office and the proper Mass of the miracle for the Turin archdiocese. In 1928 Pius XI

Interior of the Basilica of Corpus Domini

raised the Church of Corpus Domini to the dignity of a minor basilica. In the 15th century, the Holy See gave an order that the Host of the miracle be consumed, in order "not to oblige God to make the miracle eternal by keeping the Eucharistic species incorrupt forever, as is now happening."

The Eucharistic Miracle

Suddenly the bag fell open and, to the great wonder of the bystanders, the monstrance with the consecrated Host rose into the air over the surrounding houses.

The iron in which the miraculous Host had been baked was transferred to Turin from Exilles in 1673, and in 1684 it was donated to the municipality, which still keeps it among the city's historic archives.

Luigi Vacca (1853), frescoes that decorate the basilica's vault and illustrate the stages of the miracle

Box of cypress made in 1672 by the municipality of Turin to keep the documents regarding the miracle.

Plaque marking the place where the mule fell

Reproduction of the miraculous Host taken from *Il Miracolo di Torino illustrato all' occasione del primo congressa eucaristico internazionale*, Turin, Canonica Brothers Typography, 1894 (Simeon Collection, C 9200)

per non obbligare Dio a fare eterno miracolo col mantenere sempre incorrotte, come si mantennero, quelle stesse eucaristiche specie

Plaque stating that the Host of the miracle was consumed in order not to oblige God to perform an eternal miracle.

Chalice of the Miracle of Turin

To house the miraculous Host, a tabernacle was built in the cathedral in 1455. The tabernacle was removed in 1492 when construction of the new edifice, planned by Meo del Caprino, began. In 1528, on the spot where the miraculous event took place, the chapel of Matthew Sanmicheli was built. It was embellished with paintings recalling the most important events of the miracle. This edifice was later replaced by the present Church of Corpus Domini, which was begun by Ascanio Vittozzi in 1604. The building of Corpus Domini was decided by the municipality in 1598 during the plague epidemic, and also in response to a request made by the Holy Spirit Confraternity.

Anonymous, *Miracle of the Most Blessed Sacrament.* The miracle occurred in the glorious city of Turin, in the year 1453 on June 6 about 8:00 P.M., engraved plate attached to *The Secular Year* (Simeom Collection C 2412). The triptych illustrates the salient phases of the event: the stealing of the consecrated Host at Exilles, the fall of the she-mule, the ascension of the Host, and Its deposit into the chalice. The two lateral arches are surmounted by the city's coat of arms.

G.A. Recchi, frescoes illustrating the miracle, seen in Turin's city hall

During the invasion by Count d'Harcourt's army, soldiers killed many civilians in the Church of Santa Maria del Monte. The lives of the Capuchin friars, however, were spared. A French soldier broke into the tabernacle which contained a ciborium with several consecrated Hosts. Flames of fire miraculously blazed out to envelop him — burning his face and his clothing. The tabernacle door, which is adorned with agate and lapis lazzuli or blue stones, still shows the imprint of the soldier's scorched hand.

Church of the Monte dei Capuccini

*I*n 1640, the French army of Count d'Harcourt crossed the Po River and advanced to the area of the Monte dei Capuccini. Capuchin Fr. Pier Maria da Cambiano describes in great detail the Eucharistic miracle which occurred during the French troops' occupation of the Church of Santa Maria del Monte.

"The region of Piedmont was overrun with foreign troops. After Casale Monferrato was liberated from the Spaniards, the French advanced to Turin. On May 6, 1640, they arrived in Chieri; on the 7th, in Moncalieri; and on the 10th they finally reached Turin. Having occupied the left bank of the Po River, they launched an offensive attack and gained control of the bridge, despite the defense mounted by our troops, who retreated towards the convent of the Capuchins of the Monte. But even there they did not find safety. On the morning of May 12, the French launched two attacks on the trenches. They were twice repelled. On the third assault, however, our troops were compelled to lay down their arms and flee with the civilian population to seek shelter and safety in the sanctuary of a holy place, the church.

"The invaders, nevertheless, entered

Detail of the tabernacle of
the miracle

A painting of the Monte
dei Capuccini at Turin

Painting in the church
portraying the miracle

Interior of the church

the church and slaughtered men and women, young and old, civilians and troops alike, and even those who clung to the altars or who took refuge in the arms of the Capuchin friars, begging for their lives and freedom. Not one of the friars was wounded, but their hearts were broken at the sight of so much bloodshed and carnage. The soldiers destroyed sacred vessels and vestments and sacked the friary, since the refugees had stored some of their household items and furniture there for safekeeping. Afterwards, in the church itself (too horrible to recount!) they committed brutal acts of debauchery.

"As if all this were not enough, a French soldier who was a heretic climbed onto the altar and forced open the tabernacle to seize the ciborium and the Hosts it held in order to desecrate Them. But a miracle occurred! A flame blazed out of the ciborium directly towards the sacrilegious Frenchman, burning his uniform and his face. The terrified soldier threw himself to the floor, screaming and begging God's forgiveness. The church was suddenly filled with dense smoke. Between the terror and the astonishment felt by all, the vandalism ceased."

During Easter of 1570 in St. Erasmus' Church in Veroli, the Blessed Sacrament was exposed (at the time, the Blessed Sacrament was first placed in a cylindrical reliquary and then placed in a large chalice, covered with a paten) for the Forty Hours' devotion. The Child Jesus appeared in the exposed Host and granted many graces. Today, the chalice in which the Blessed Sacrament was exposed is kept in the same church and is used once a year for the celebration of Mass on Easter Tuesday.

A print depicting the miracle

At Easter in 1570 in St. Erasmus' Church, the consecrated Host, according to the traditional rite at the time, was placed in a cylindrical reliquary with a hinged cover, which was then placed in a large chalice covered by a paten. The chalice was covered by an elegant silk veil. (It should be mentioned that at that time, exposition of the Blessed Sacrament in a monstrance was not a widespread practice, even though the Council of Cologne in 1452 had specifically mentioned the monstrance.)

It was the custom that each confraternity in the city would be present for an hour of adoration before the exposed Blessed Sacrament. Thus, those enrolled in the Confraternity of Mercy (which predated

both the Confraternity of Corpus Christi and that of our Blessed Lady), vested in their black robes, were all kneeling in prayer.

The most authentic document regarding this Eucharistic miracle was drawn up immediately by the chancery. It is preserved in the archives of St. Erasmus' Church. A very detailed deposition and account of the miraculous event is given by a Giacomo Meloni, who was among the first witnesses of the miracle. His testimony follows: "Raising my eyes towards the chalice, I saw a most brilliant star on its base, and above the star, the Blessed Sacrament, the same size as the Host used by the priest at Mass. The star was attached to the Blessed Sacrament (...).

The chalice and paten of the miracle

St. Erasmus Church, Veroli

The chapel where the apparition occurred

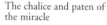

The document which records the sworn and written testimony of the witnesses who were present at the apparition

The vision ended when small children in adoration, similar to small angels, were seen around the Sacred Host...."

To this day, this miraculous event is commemorated every Easter Tuesday with solemn ceremonies in which the Bishop takes part.

The chalice, its paten, and the silver pyx in which the Blessed Sacrament was exposed have all been preserved along with some saints' reliquaries. The miraculous Host of Veroli was consumed about 112 years after the miracle occurred.

In 1970, on the fourth centenary of the miracle, the Third Eucharistic Congress of the diocese of Veroli-Frosinone was

IL 26 MARZO 1570 SOLENNITA DI PASQUA
L'OSTIA SACROSANTA
RACCHIUSA IN DUPLICE CUSTODIA ARGENTEA
RAVVOLTA IN DRAPPO SERICO LEGATO
PER VIVISSIMA LUCE DI STELLA RAGGIANTE
E SORREGGENTE IL SSMO SACRAMENTO
SI RESE VISIBILE AGLI ADORATORI
QUINDI SI CONVERTÍ IN VEZZOSO BAMBINO
ELEVANTESI SULLA SOMMITA DEL CALICE
TRA NUVOLETTA E SOVRUMANI SPLENDORI

The commemorative tablet recalling the miracle

celebrated. Adoration of the Blessed Sacrament takes place every First Friday in the church of the Eucharistic miracle, while all the other churches are closed.

In 1472, during the war between Volterra and Florence, a Florentine soldier stole a precious ivory ciborium containing numerous consecrated Hosts from the cathedral in Volterra. As soon as he left the church, in a fit of fury against the Sacramental Jesus, he threw the Ciborium with its precious Contents against one of the outer walls. All the Hosts fell out, and, illuminated by a mysterious light, rose into the air and remained suspended for a long time. There were many eyewitnesses of this prodigy.

Some of the principal causes of the pointless Allumiere war, which ended with the sacking of Volterra in 1472 by the Duke of Montefeltro's army, were the tension between the different social classes and the personal interests of Lorenzo de Medici. Absorbed by the Florentine state, Volterra was subjected to harsh treatment, which caused the emigration of many wealthy families and the appropriation of their goods at bankruptcy prices.

It was in this historical context that this Eucharistic miracle took place in 1472.

Among the most authoritative accounts describing the miracle, we have the written account of Friar Biagio Lisci, who was an eyewitness. The account is now kept in the archives of St. Francis' Church. We also have some writings preserved in the municipal library of Volterra. A Florentine soldier entered the cathedral and went directly to the tabernacle, from which he took the ciborium containing consecrated Hosts, along with many other sacred objects. As soon as he left the church, filled with a deep hatred of Jesus in the Eucharist, the soldier flung the ciborium against one of the external walls.

Interior of the cathedral

Church of St. Francis

View of Volterra

All the Hosts fell out, and, as if held by an invisible hand, rose into the air, all radiant with light. The soldier fell to the ground with fright, and, repentant, began to weep. There were many eyewitnesses of this marvel.

City panorama

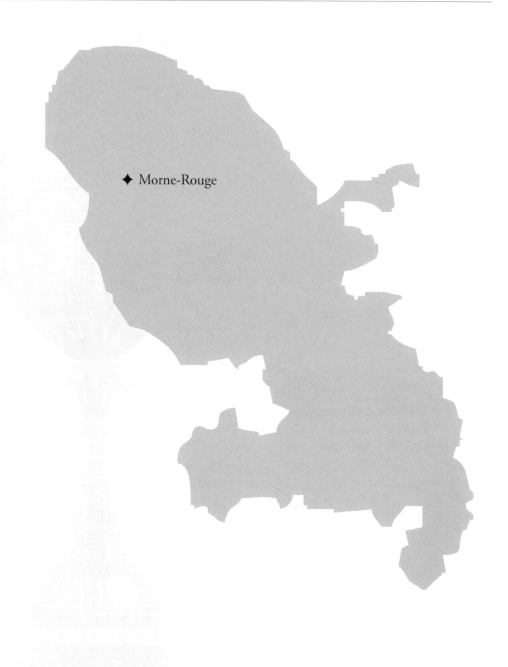

♦ Morne-Rouge

On May 8, 1902, the Mt. Pelée volcano suddenly erupted. Molten lava immediately reached the nearby city of Saint-Pierre de la Martinique and completely destroyed it, while the eruption mysteriously spared the village of Morne-Rouge, which was right near the volcano's peak. The prodigious event was accompanied by an apparition of Jesus and His Sacred Heart in the Host exposed for public Eucharistic adoration. There were many witnesses to this extraordinary phenomenon.

On May 8, 1902, Ascension Day, the Mt. Pelée volcano began spewing lava and ashes. The inhabitants of Morne-Rouge, who had a strong devotion to the Sacred Heart of Jesus, immediately hurried to their parish church to ask Our Lady of Deliverance to spare their village from catastrophe.

At that moment of imminent danger, those who were estranged from one another sought reconciliation, and people began to confess their sins. The parish priest, Fr. Mary, gave general absolution to all the faithful, distributed Holy Communion, and then exposed the Blessed Sacrament for public adoration. At a certain point, a woman cried out, "The Sacred Heart of Jesus is in the Host!" A large number of people witnessed the apparition of Jesus in the Host, showing His Sacred Heart crowned with thorns. Some declared that they also saw the Precious Blood of Jesus dripping from His Sacred Heart. The vision lasted several hours and ended only after the reposition of the Blessed Sacrament in the tabernacle. On May 8th, the village of Morne-Rouge was spared from the volcano's devastating fury. Therefore, the local population had a chance to reconcile with God, receive the sacra-

Parish church of Morne-
Rouge

View of Morne-Rouge

ments, and so be prepared to die in the state of grace. On August 30th of the same year, a violent eruption of the same volcano destroyed the village of Morne-Rouge.

Alkmaar

Amsterdam

Boxtel-Hoogstraten

Breda-Niervaart

Boxmeer

Bergen

Stiphout

Meerssen

In 1429 in Alkmaar's Cathedral of St. Lawrence, a priest, Fr. Folkert, was celebrating his first Mass. After the Consecration, the priest accidentally knocked the chalice over, spilling consecrated Wine on the altar and on his chasuble. The Wine was miraculously transformed into Blood. Every attempt to remove the traces of Blood from the chasuble was in vain. The precious reliquary of the chasuble soaked in Blood is preserved to this day in the Cathedral of St. Lawrence in Alkmaar.

DE ENGEL VAN HET H. BLOED-MIRAKEL

Courtesy of the Meertens Institute

*I*n the Cathedral of St. Lawrence in Alkmaar there is a precious reliquary shaped like an angel, containing a chasuble soaked in Blood from the Eucharistic miracle of 1429.

On May 1, 1429, a priest named Fr. Folkert was celebrating his first Mass in the Cathedral of St. Lawrence. The pastor, Fr. Volpert Schult, assisted. Shortly after having pronounced the words of consecration, Fr. Folkert inadvertently knocked over the chalice containing white consecrated Wine, which splashed onto his chasuble and turned into living Blood. After Mass, in a state of panic, the new priest cut off the part of the chasuble spotted with Blood and burned it. He then took the remaining piece and began to sew it up. But as soon as he finished mending the chasuble, the Blood spots reappeared. The two priests, not knowing what to do, immediately took the chasuble to the Bishop of Utrecht. In 1433, after numerous canonical investigations, the Bishop officially approved devotion to this miracle.

Church interior

Procession in honor of the miracle

Church of St. Lawrence

Reliquary containing the Blood of the miracle

Painting in the church depicting the miracle

In Amsterdam, a consecrated Host was miraculously preserved from flames. Ysbrand Dommer was gravely ill and vomited a Host he had received. His maid threw the Holy Eucharist into the lit fireplace. The consecrated Host was found the next day, completely intact and suspended in the air inside the fireplace. There were many witnesses of the miracle, and the Bishop of Utrecht, Jan van Arkel, immediately authorized its veneration. Even today in Amsterdam there is a yearly procession in honor of the miracle.

The nine panels on which the painter, C. Schenk, depicted the scenes of the miracle

On March 12, 1345, a few days before Easter, Ysbrand Dommer, thinking he was near death, sent for the parish priest of Oude Kerk so he could receive the Last Rites. Shortly after receiving Holy Communion, he vomited everything into a small basin, whose contents were then thrown into the flames of the fireplace.

The next day Ysbrand was completely restored to health. One of the maids taking care of him went to stir up the fire and noticed a strange light with a Host in the middle. The woman began to scream, and everyone within earshot ran to witness the miracle. Ysbrand took the Host and wrapped It in a linen cloth, placed It in a case and immediately carried It to the parish priest. But the miracle continued: three times the priest had to return to Ysbrand's house to take back the Host, which had miraculously reappeared there. It was then decided to turn Ysbrand Dommer's house into a chapel.

On Easter Sunday, everyone who had witnessed the miracle, along with the mayor of Amstel, compiled an accurate

Painting depicting the miracle

Painting showing a solemn procession in honor of the miracle

Ysbrand Dommer receiving Communion

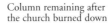

Column remaining after the church burned down

Lamp in which the Blessed Sacrament is depicted in honor of the first *Stille Omgang* procession

account of the events. The report was delivered to the Bishop of Utrecht, Jan van Arkel, who authorized devotion to the miracle.

In 1452 the chapel was destroyed by a fire, but strangely, the monstrance containing the miraculous Host remained intact. In 1665 the city council authorized Father Jan Van der Mey to convert one of the houses of the former convent of the Beghines into a chapel. Here the precious monstrance was transferred, but unfortunately was shortly afterwards stolen by unknown thieves.

Even today there is perpetual exposition of the Blessed Sacrament in memory of the miracle. The only objects which remain from the Eucharistic miracle are the case which contained the Host, the documents which describe the miracle, and some paintings housed in the Historical Museum of Amsterdam. Every year on the eve of Palm Sunday there is a silent procession *(Stille Omgang)* in honor of the miracle.

The Eucharistic Miracle

In 1452 the chapel was destroyed by a fire, but strangely, the monstrance containing the miraculous Host remained intact.

Stille Omgang procession held each year in honor of the miracle

The chapel of the church was destroyed again in 1908

Archduke Maximilian of Austria portrayed in adoration before the reliquary of the miraculous Host (1484)

Nun of the Order of Beghines

Nieuwezijds, an old print of the Chapel of the Miracle (1670)

Modern representation of the miracle

First chapel of the Beghines, 1397

Facade of the current church of Beghine, Amsterdam

Sculpture showing the monstrance which contained the miraculous Host

Painting depicting the miracle

Pamphlet from the *Stille Omgang* procession

Interior of the church

Tablet describing the miracle

Chapel of the Most Blessed Sacrament

The city of Bergen is famous not only for its characteristic canals but also for a Eucharistic miracle which took place there in 1421. For many months, the pastor of the Church of Sts. Peter and Paul had experienced doubts about whether the Body and Blood of Christ were truly present in the consecrated Host. The priest showed no devotion towards the Blessed Sacrament, to the point that one day after celebrating Mass he took the leftover consecrated Hosts and threw Them into the river. Some months later the Hosts were found, floating in the water and soaked in Blood.

*B*ergen op Zoom (City on the Border) is located along the estuary of the Schelda River and has many canals running across it. In 1421, on the Sunday before the feast of Pentecost, the pastor of the Church of Sts. Peter and Paul, not believing the truth of transubstantiation, threw some consecrated Hosts (left over from Mass) into the canal.

Several months later, some fishermen found the Hosts floating in the water and soaked in coagulated Blood. News of the miraculous finding of the Hosts spread quickly, and immediately many pilgrims came to see the marvel. Devotion was approved by the Bishop and, though it was banned for a long period during the Protestant Reformation, Catholics silently continued to keep alive the memory of the miracle. Devotion was restored in the 20th century, and there are numerous public events to commemorate the miracle.

KORTE
BESCHRIJVING

VAN HET
MIRAKEL VAN HET H. BLOED
VAN
BERGEN
IN NOORDHOLLAND

Painting depicting the
procession in honor of the
miracle, Meertens Institut

View of the Schelda
River

The Church of Sts.
Peter and Paul and the
Schelda River

A small-scale model of
Bergen at the time of the
miracle

Jules Breton, *Procession of the Blessed Sacrament*, 1857

During a Mass in Boxmeer, Holland, in the year 1400, the species of wine was transformed into Blood and bubbled out of the chalice, splashing onto the corporal. The priest, terrified at the sight, asked God to forgive his doubts, and the Blood immediately stopped bubbling out of the chalice. The Blood that had fallen onto the corporal coagulated into a lump the size of a walnut. Even today one can see the Blood, which has not changed at all over time.

Stained glass window depicting the miracle

The Eucharistic miracle of Boxmeer took place in the Church of Sts. Peter and Paul in 1400. Father Arnoldus Groen was celebrating Mass. Immediately after having consecrated the Eucharistic species, the priest doubted the Real Presence of the Lord in the consecrated Bread and Wine. Without warning, the consecrated Wine, as though the Precious Blood were boiling, began bubbling out of the chalice and onto the corporal.

The Wine was changed into Blood and coagulated in a great lump. The relics of the corporal and the Precious Blood are preserved to this day, and the anniversary of the miracle is celebrated with a solemn annual procession. There are many documents describing the miracle, among which are many stone tablets and paintings. Popes Clement XI, Benedict XIV, Pius IX and Leo XIII all showed particular devotion to this miracle.

Procession in honor of the miracle

Church of Sts. Peter and Paul at Boxmeer

Interior of the church

Reliquary of the Blood

Boxtel is particularly famous for a Eucharistic miracle which occurred there around the year 1380. A priest named Eligius van der Aker was celebrating Mass at the altar of the Three Kings. Immediately after the Consecration, he accidentally knocked over the chalice containing consecrated white Wine, which immediately changed into Blood and stained the corporal and the altar cloth. The relic of the Blood-stained corporal is still kept in Boxtel, while the altar cloth was given to the town of Hoogstraten. The most authoritative document describing the miracle is a decree issued in 1380 by Cardinal Pileus.

A depiction of the miracle

*I*n 1380, the priest Eligius van der Aker was celebrating Mass in St. Peter's Church. Shortly after consecrating the species of wine, he inadvertently spilled the Precious Blood onto the corporal and altar cloth. Although he had used white wine for the Mass, it turned into Blood.

At the end of Mass the priest ran into the sacristy and tried to remove the Blood stains from the sacred linens, but all his attempts were in vain. Not knowing what to do, he hid the altar cloth and corporal in a valise under his bed. Only when he was dying did he reveal the secret to his confessor, Fr. Henrijk van Meerheim. The latter immediately informed Cardinal Pileus, who at the time was the apostolic legate of Pope Urban VI and titular of the Church of St. Praxedes. After conducting a thorough investigation into what had happened, the Cardinal authorized veneration of the relics by a decree dated June 25, 1380. Due to religious

Exterior of St. Catherine's Church, Hoogstraten

Relic of the Miraculous Blood, St. Catherine's Church

The relic being carried in procession

The Eucharistic miracle took place at St. Peter's Church in Boxtel

conflicts, the relics were moved in 1652 to Hoogstraten on the Belgian border. Only in 1924, after repeated requests, was the Blood-stained corporal returned to the little town of Boxtel. Every year on the Feast of the Blessed Trinity, the people of Boxtel organize a solemn procession commemorating the Eucharistic miracle and expose the relic for public veneration.

The Eucharistic Miracle

Although the priest had used white wine for the Mass, it was transformed into Blood.

Depictions of the miracle

Courtesy of the Meertens Institute

A painting in the church depicting the miracle

Interior of the church

Relic of the Blood-stained corporal

The Eucharistic miracle of Breda-Niervaart occurred on June 24, 1300. At the time, the Netherlands were occupied by Spanish troops. During a raid, a soldier stole a consecrated Host, which was found a short while later by a farmer named Jan Bautoen. The Host had been hidden under a lump of dirt and was in perfect condition. One of the most authoritative and complete documents describing the events connected with this miracle is the investigation conducted by the Bishop of Link. Traces of the miracle remain in the church's paintings as well as in the documents.

*O*n June 24, 1300, a farmer named Jan Bautoen was hoeing a plot of land near the village of Niervaart. As he lifted a clod of earth, he found a completely intact Host, which he immediately brought to the pastor of Niervaart. The Host was placed in a precious container, and despite the passage of time, one could see that the species of the bread remained intact. News quickly spread among the people, who began to venerate the Host. In 1449 the Holy Eucharist was moved to the Collegiate Church of Our Lady of Breda, and an artistic monstrance was made in which to preserve the Blessed Sacrament.

During the religious conflicts, all traces of the miraculous Host were unfortunately lost, even though devotion to this Eucharistic miracle was kept alive by the people. Veneration was solemnly restored in the 20th century by a confraternity in Breda dedicated to the Blessed Sacrament. To this day, processions and public prayers in honor of the miracle are held each year on the Feast of Corpus Christi.

The procession held every year to honor the miracle

Interior of the church

Artistic monstrance in which the miraculous Host is carried in procession, Breda

Banner depicting the finding of the miraculous Host

Courtesy of the Meertens Institute

Collegiate Church of Our Lady, Breda

The relic of the miraculous Host is carried in procession (1535), Sacred Museum of Breda

The relic of this Eucharistic miracle can be venerated even today in Spain. It is kept at the Royal Monastery of El Escorial, although the miracle took place in Holland. Some Protestant mercenaries entered the Catholic church in Gorkum, Holland, and plundered it. As an insult, one of them trampled a consecrated Host with a spiked boot, perforating the Host in three places. Live Blood immediately began to drip from the holes, which took on the form of three small wounds in a circle. These marks are still visible today.

The *Sagrada Forma* exposed in the Gothic temple

The *Sagrada Forma* (Sacred Form) is still intact and is venerated even today in the sacristy of the Royal Monastery of San Lorenzo in El Escorial (near Madrid). It was desecrated in Gorkum (in Holland) in 1572 by followers of Ulrich Zwingli called the "Sea Beggers," who were in the pay of the Prince of Orange.

After invading the city, the conquerors began to loot it, not sparing even the cathedral. In fact, as soon as they entered, they began striking the tabernacle with iron bars, seizing from it the monstrance containing the Blessed Sacrament. The Host was then thrown onto the ground and trampled with a spiked boot which pierced It in three places. Immediately Blood began to ooze from these three holes, and the holes took on the form of three small wounds in a circle, as can still be seen today. One of the desecrators, shocked at the sight and repentant, brought the news to Canon Jean van der Delft, who managed to save the Host.

The relic was eventually given to King Philip II of Spain in 1594, who placed It in the care of the Monastery of San Lorenzo in El Escorial. Above the

The altar where the painting depicting the *Sagrada Forma* is kept

Detail of the painting by Claudio Coello

The church where the miracle took place in Holland

Gothic temple designed by Vincente Lopez

King Philip II

The *Sagrada Forma*

Procession in honor of the miracle – court dignitaries in adoration before the *Sagrada Forma*

Painting by Claudio Coello commissioned by Carlos II

altar where the miraculous Host is preserved, the Italian artist Filippo Filippini made four marble and bronze bas-reliefs representing the miraculous events. The painting by Claudio Coello (1621–1693) shows the inauguration of the magnificent tabernacle commissioned by King Charles II specifically to contain the precious relic. In El Escorial on September 29th and October 28th, in remembrance of the miracle, there are solemn festivities in which the precious Host, known by the name of *Sagrada Forma*, is exposed and carried in procession.

View of the Royal Monastery of El Escorial

Courtyard of the Church of the Royal Monastery of El Escorial

In 1222 and 1465, two important Eucharistic miracles took place in the town of Meerssen. The first occurred during Holy Mass, when living Blood dripped from the large Host and stained the corporal. The second occurred in 1456, when a farmer managed to rescue the relic of the miracle from a fire that had destroyed the whole church. The church was later rebuilt, and in 1938 Pope Pius XI raised it to the status of minor basilica. Numerous pilgrims come to Meerssen every year to venerate the relic of the miracle.

Basilica of the Blessed Sacrament, Meerssen

The ancient chapel of Meerssen, thanks in part to Gerberga of Saxony, wife of the French King Louis IV d'Outremer, was enlarged in the mid-tenth century and became an important church. In 1222, an important Eucharistic miracle occurred in this church and was recognized by the ecclesiastical authorities. During the celebration of Sunday Mass, after the priest consecrated the Eucharistic species, living Blood started to drip from the large Host, staining the corporal.

In 1465 a huge fire broke out and destroyed the church, but a farmer managed to rescue the relic of the Blood-stained Host, which remained completely unharmed. The townspeople remember this episode as the "Miracle of the Fire." The church was immediately rebuilt, and in 1938 Pius XI elevated it to the status of minor basilica. Today it is still a major pilgrimage center in the Netherlands, and the precious relic of the miracle is carried in procession each year during the octave of Corpus Christi.

Interior of the basilica

Altar of the miracle

Medals commemorating the miracle

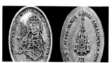

View of the Basilica

A painting in the basilica depicting the miracle

NOVEENBOEKJE

VAN HET H. SACRAMENT
VAN MIRAKEL

BASILIEK MEERSSEN

In the village of Stiphout, some consecrated Hosts were preserved from a raging fire that destroyed the whole church, which was later rebuilt. In addition to the many documents describing the miracle, there is a painting depicting the miraculous event in the parish church where it occurred. This event is celebrated each year by the residents of Stiphout, especially on the Feast of Corpus Christi.

Picture showing the miracle. In the background Jan Balloys is seen rescuing the Blessed Sacrament.

*I*n 1342 a violent thunderstorm suddenly broke out in the village of Stiphout. A lightning bolt struck the parish church, setting it on fire. The flames quickly spread everywhere and reached the interior of the church. Not knowing what to do, the elderly pastor, Jan Hocaerts, immediately ran to warn the neighbors. A group of the faithful, led by Jan Balloys, decided to try to rescue the Blessed Sacrament.

It was impossible to enter the church, and the only solution left was for someone to be lowered down through the window. Jan Balloys volunteered. After breaking the glass of the large window near the altar with a bar, he let himself down inside. With great amazement, he saw that the flames, which had already destroyed the whole church, had held back from the area around the tabernacle. Jan then opened the tabernacle, grabbed the ciborium containing the consecrated Hosts, and carried Them to safety. Everyone immediately shouted, "Miracle!"

The church was later rebuilt, and the Hosts remained intact until 1557. Because of historical vicissitudes and religious wars, every trace of Them was subsequently lost.

St. Trudo's Church, Stiphout

Interior of St. Trudo's Church

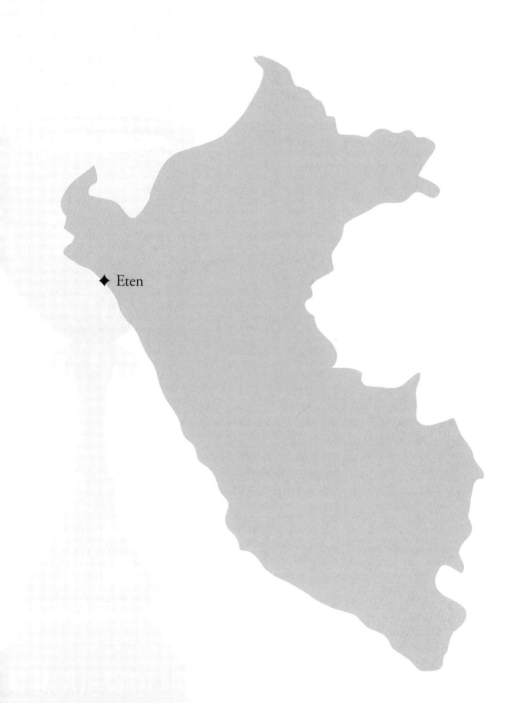

The Eucharistic miracle of Eten happened over 350 years ago in the Peruvian town of Port Eten. In a Host exposed for public adoration, the Child Jesus and three interconnected hearts of a brilliant white color appeared. Every year, the feast in honor of this event begins on July 12, with the transfer of the *Divino Niño* (Divine Child) statue from its shrine to its temple in the city of Eten, and ends on July 24.

Image of the Divine Child of Eten

*T*he first apparition of the Divine Child in the Most Blessed Sacrament took place on the night of June 2, 1649, during Vespers and solemn exposition in honor of the Feast of Corpus Christi. At the end of the service, the Franciscan friar, Fr. Jerome de Silva Manrique, was about to return the monstrance to the tabernacle, but he suddenly stopped. In the Host there had appeared the radiant face of a Child, framed by thick, light brown curls falling to the shoulders. All the faithful present in the church saw the same vision.

The second apparition took place a few days later, on July 22nd of the same year, during a celebration in honor of St. Mary Magdalene, patroness of the city. According to the testimony of Br. Marco Lopez, superior of the convent in Chiclayo, during exposition of the Most Blessed Sacrament, "the Divine Child Jesus again appeared in the Host, dressed in a purple tunic. Beneath it he wore a shirt up to the middle of the chest, according to the custom of the South American Indians." Through this sign, the Divine Child wanted to identify with the native inhabitants of Eten to demonstrate His love for them.

Colca Valley

Lake Titicaca

Ancient terraces,
Peru

Celebrations in honor of the Divine Child

In the same apparition, which lasted about 15 minutes, many also saw appearing in the Host three small white hearts joined to each other. These symbolized the Three Persons of the Blessed Trinity: the Father, the Son, and the Holy Spirit, present in the consecrated Host. To this day, the yearly feast in honor of the miracle of the Divine Child of Eten continues to attract thousands of the faithful.

Machu Picchu (Inca City)

♦ Glotowo

♦ Poznan

♦ Krakow

In 1290, Lithuanian troops invaded Poland. A priest from the Polish village of Glotowo buried a gold-plated silver ciborium in a field. Inside the ciborium was a consecrated Host which he had left there by mistake. The Lithuanian troops destroyed the village and the church. None of the survivors knew about the hidden Host. Only a number of years later, while plowing the field in the spring, a farmer found the ciborium by chance, thanks to the strange behavior of his oxen. They had bowed to the ground in adoration of the Host, which was emitting a very bright light.

The oldest documents describing this miracle narrate that "some oxen were pulling a plow, behind which a farmer was walking. The sun was setting on the horizon, creating long shadows. The man lifted his eyes and prodded the animals which, after a long day's work, were going slowly up the hill. *After so much work,* the farmer thought, *we will have bread.* All of a sudden, the plow got stuck, the oxen pulled harder, and on the side they turned over a big clod of earth.

"The animals stopped as if frozen. At first the farmer scolded the beasts, yet he paused, surprised at the sudden change in the atmosphere around him. The field was lit up as if it were noon, and a very intense light was coming from the ground, shining on the kneeling oxen. The farmer began to dig and noticed that the bright light was coming from a little ciborium covered with dirt. It contained a perfect Host as white as snow."

News of the extraordinary event spread rapidly among the people, who immediately rushed to the site. The local authorities organized a solemn procession to bring the Host to the church

The Eucharistic shrine of Glotowo

The ciborium containing the miraculous Host. To the sides are seen the oxen which were found kneeling in the field adoring the Host

Interior of the shrine

in Dobre Miasto, though according to an old chronicle, inexplicably, the Host disappeared and was found at the same spot as the first time. The event was interpreted as a sign from above, and a little church dedicated to Corpus Christi was built on that spot.

The popularity of Glotowo grew through the centuries, and in the 18th century the old medieval church was enlarged and consecrated by Bishop Krzysztof Potocki on July 24, 1726. Even today, every year the shrine of Glotowo attracts numerous pilgrims who come to venerate the Host, which has remained intact since 1290.

The Eucharistic miracle of Krakow consisted of consecrated Hosts which emitted an unusual bright light when they were hidden by thieves in a muddy swamp. The thieves had stolen a ciborium containing consecrated Hosts from a church in the village of Wawel (outside of modern-day Krakow). Eventually they abandoned the ciborium and Hosts in a marsh outside the village, where the miracle took place. Corpus Christi Church in Krakow, Poland, contains paintings depicting the miracle, as well as documents and depositions relating to the matter.

A representation of the procession of the Bishop back into the city after finding the Hosts of the miracle in the marsh

*I*n the year 1345, King Casimar III the Great of Poland gave orders that a church named Corpus Christi be built in honor of the Eucharistic miracle which had taken place that same year. It happened in the village of Wawel, near Krakow. Some thieves had broken into a little church (the Collegiate Church of All Saints) which was a short distance from Krakow. They forced their way into the tabernacle and stole the ciborium containing consecrated Hosts. But when they figured out that the ciborium was not made of real gold, they threw it, along with the Hosts, into a muddy swamp filled with garbage.

Immediately a mysterious light began to emanate from the spot where the treasure had been abandoned. The bright flashes lasted continuously for several days. The whole village witnessed the strange phenomenon and unanimously decided to inform the Bishop of Krakow. The Bishop, not understanding how such intense flashes of light could be coming from a marsh, called for three days of fasting and prayer. On the third day, he led the whole village in procession out to the marsh. There they found the ciborium, and within it they found the Hosts, completely intact and radiating the unusual flashes of light. The people,

Corpus Christi Church, Krakow

View of the Wawel area where the miracle took place, now completely developed

King Casimir III the Great

Inside Corpus Christi Church, Krakow

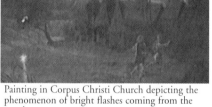

Painting in Corpus Christi Church depicting the phenomenon of bright flashes coming from the marsh

Detail of the painting

moved to tears, began to pray and celebrate the miracle. Annually on the feast of Corpus Christi, the miracle is commemorated at the Church of Corpus Christi in Krakow.

In 1399 in the city of Poznan, some desecrators stole three consecrated Hosts and, out of contempt, pierced Them with pointed instruments. At once, Blood began dripping from the Hosts. Every attempt to destroy Them was useless. To avoid discovery of their crime, the scoundrels decided to throw the Holy Eucharist into a swamp. But the Hosts rose into the air, emitting powerful rays of light. Only after ardent prayer was the Bishop able to recover the Hosts, which can be venerated to this very day in the Church of Corpus Domini in Poznan.

The stained glass window in which the three miraculous Hosts are depicted

*I*n 1399, in the city of Poznan, profaners with an intense hatred for the Christian faith persuaded a servant girl to take three consecrated Hosts from the Dominican (now Jesuit) church. The woman, enticed by a large reward, succeeded in stealing three Hosts. Immediately after they received the Hosts, the malefactors went to the basement of their mansion, put the Hosts on a table and desecrated the Eucharist, piercing the Hosts with pointed instruments. Suddenly, a copious amount of Blood began to drip from the Hosts and splashed onto the face of a girl afflicted with blindness, and she immediately regained her sight. The desecrators, seized with panic and

anxiety, tried to destroy the Hosts, which nevertheless remained whole. Unable to rid themselves of the Holy Eucharist, they decided to take the Hosts outside the city and throw Them into a marsh near the Warta River.

A young shepherd who happened to be passing near the marsh saw the three luminous Hosts suspended in the air. Trying to contain his emotion, he returned home and recounted everything to his father and the local authorities. The burgomaster was indifferent to the young man's account and, believing him to be an imposter, ordered that he be jailed. The young shepherd mysteriously managed to escape and

Eucharistic shrine

At the Eucharistic shrine, the precious monstrances donated by King Wladyslaw Jagiello are preserved and are still used for exposition of the Blessed Sacrament

again presented himself to the burgo-master, who, finally convinced of the facts, made his way to the place of the miracle. In the meantime, the entire population had gathered around the three luminous Hosts suspended in the air. Only Bishop Wojciech Jastrzebiec, after beseeching Heaven with fervent prayers, succeeded in retrieving the Hosts, which descended into the pyx in his hands. The Bishop immediately directed that a solemn procession be formed to accompany the miraculous Hosts to St. Mary Magdalene Church.

At the site of the miracle, a wooden chapel was constructed which became the goal of many pilgrimages. King Wladyslaw Jagiello came to know of the miracle and made a journey to Poznan to venerate the miraculous Hosts. As a sign of devotion, the king ordered that a church dedicated to the Body of Christ (Corpus Domini) be built on the exact spot where the miracle occurred. In the 19th century, in place of the old mansion where the profanation of the Hosts took place, a shrine was constructed where even today the table with the imprints from the Blood that dripped from the Hosts has been preserved. Every Thursday a procession with the Blessed Sacrament takes place at the Church of Corpus Domini to recall the miracle.

The Eucharistic Miracle

Suddenly, a copious amount of Blood began to drip from the Hosts and splashed onto the face of a girl afflicted with blindness, and she immediately regained her sight.

A fresco on the sacristy ceiling of the Eucharistic shrine, in which a scene from the miracle is represented

The sacristy of the Eucharistic shrine constructed around the middle of the 18th century

In the central nave, under the altar where the relics of St. Onufry are preserved, three 18th century sculptures are preserved which depict the desecrators who tried to get rid of the Hosts

The interior of the shrine

The original chapel in which the miraculous Hosts were preserved up until the last century

♦ Santarém

The Eucharistic miracle of Santarém, together with that of Lanciano, is considered to be among the most important Eucharistic miracles. Numerous studies and canonical analyses were carried out on the relics. The Host changed into bleeding Flesh, and Blood flowed from the Blessed Sacrament. Both relics are preserved to this day in St. Stephen's Church in Santarém. The couple's home became a chapel in 1684.

Relic of the miraculous Host

Several Popes granted plenary indulgences to this Eucharistic miracle: Pius IV, St. Pius V, Pius VI, and Gregory XIV. Still today in St. Stephen's Church in Santarém, one can venerate these precious relics.

According to the date recorded in the document commissioned by King Alphonsus IV in 1346, on February 16, 1266, in Santarém, a young woman, overcome with jealousy for her husband, consulted a sorceress who told her to go to the church and steal a consecrated Host to use for a love potion. The woman stole the Host and hid It in a linen cloth which immediately became stained with Blood. Frightened by this, she ran home and opened the kerchief to see what had happened. To her amazement, she saw that Blood was dripping from the Host. The confused woman stored the Host in a drawer in her bedroom. That night the drawer began to emit brilliant rays of light which illuminated the room as if it were daytime. The husband was also aware of the strange phenomenon and questioned his wife, who was obliged to tell him everything.

The next day, the couple informed the pastor, who went to their home to remove the Host and return It to St. Stephen's Church in solemn procession, accompanied by many religious and lay people. The Host bled for three consecutive days. Later It was placed

Interior of the church

Cruet containing the Blood from the Host

Interior of the Shrine of the *Santíssimo Milagre*, Santarém

House where the miracle occurred

Altar where the relic of the miracle is preserved

Shrine of the *Santíssimo Milagre*, Santarém

in a beautiful reliquary made of beeswax.

In 1340 another miracle occurred. When the priest opened the tabernacle, he found the beeswax vase broken into many pieces: in its place was a crystal vase containing the Blood mixed with the wax.

The Sacred Host is now preserved in an 18th-century Eucharistic throne above the main altar. St. Stephen's Church is now known as the Shrine of the Holy Miracle. Throughout the centuries, on various occasions the Host bled again, and on occasion different images of Our Lord were seen in the Holy Eucharist. Among the witnesses of this prodigy was St. Francis Xavier, the apostle to the Indies, who visited the shrine before leaving for the missions. Every year since the miracle occurred, on the second Sunday of April, the precious relic has been carried in procession from the couple's home to St. Stephen's Church.

The woman stole the Host and hid It in a linen cloth which immediately became stained with Blood.

A witch counsels the woman to steal a consecrated Host

The woman receives Communion and steals the Host

Pedro Crasbeeck, print from 1612 showing the glass ampulla in which the Host of the miracle was miraculously found

The woman's husband discovers the theft, noticing that rays of light are coming from the kitchen cabinet. He opens the cabinet and sees a bloody Host which has changed into Flesh

Commemorative medallion of the Miracle of Santarém

The local authorities rush to return the miraculous Host to the church

The sacrilegious woman's home which was converted into a small chapel, Santarém

- ✦ O'Cebreiro
- ✦ Ponferrada
- San Juan de las Abadesas ✦
- Ivorra ✦ Gerona
- ✦ Zaragoza ✦ ✦ Montserrat
- Cimballa ✦ ✦ Daroca
- ✦ El Escorial
- ✦ Alcalá
- ✦ Guadalupe
- Moncada
- Valencia ✦ Alboraya-Almácera
- ✦ Silla
- ✦ Alcoy
- ✦ Onil
- ✦ Caravaca de la Cruz

In 1348, a priest on his way to bring Communion to some sick people slipped into a small river he was crossing and dropped the ciborium containing some consecrated Hosts. The poor priest had resigned himself to the loss when he heard some fishermen a short distance away calling to him, asking him to come to the shore to see several fish with disks in their mouths which looked like Hosts. The Hosts were immediately brought back to the church in a solemn procession in which the whole village participated.

Sculpture commemorating the miracle

*I*n 1348, in the town of Alboraya-Almácera, a Eucharistic miracle occurred which brings to mind episodes in the life of Saint Francis. These events show how, if men were to fully live in the grace of God, all creatures would live in harmony.

A priest, carrying a ciborium containing Viaticum (the Eucharist) destined for some sick people, was crossing a river on mule-back when he was suddenly swept off his mount by a rushing wave. The priest tumbled into the water along with his ciborium, which was emptied of its precious Contents.

The Hosts fell out and were carried away by the current toward the mouth of the river nearby. The priest, who barely escaped being drowned, heard the voices of some fishermen calling to him to come and see, "in the place where the waters of the river mix with those of the sea," three fish, each with a little white disk in its mouth. The fishermen were very perplexed because the three disks looked like Communion Hosts.

The priest immediately ran to the church and returned to the river bank with another ciborium. He was in

Hermitage Church in Alboraya

such a hurry that he didn't even stop to wonder whether the fishermen's story was believable. Great was his joy when he saw that the three remarkable fish were there, almost completely out of the water, lifting the Hosts intact with their mouths, like little trophies. He fell to his knees, and holding out the chalice, prayed as he had never prayed before in his entire life; then, he saw the fish deposit the Hosts into the chalice, one after the other, and then dive and slither rapidly back into the water to disappear into the sea. Only at that moment did the priest notice that he was surrounded by a group of people who had witnessed the entire scene.

Today one can still consult numerous documents testifying to the miracle. There is a small church, with two fish carved on the door, built on the site of the miracle, and two paintings depicting the entire event.

Great was his joy when he saw that the three remarkable fish were there, almost completely out of the water, lifting the Hosts intact with their mouths, like little trophies.

Interior of the parish church of Almácera

River crossed by the priest in the Sierra Calderone

Commemorative tablet

Commemorative candle of the fish of Alboraya-Almácera.

Mosaic on the exterior of the church

The fish place the Sacred Hosts in the chalice. The present fresco in the parish church of Almácera

The procession held every year on the feast of Corpus Christi to commemorate the miracle

The miraculous fish are represented on the doors to the church

Detail of the main entrance to the church constructed in memory of the miracle

ALCALÁ

In the year 1597, a thief stole some consecrated Hosts along with some precious objects from a church not far from Alcalá, Spain. A few days later, the thief returned, full of profound remorse, and confessed his sins at the Jesuit church. The priest who heard his confession had him return the Hosts; however, for the sake of prudence, the priest decided to keep the Hosts in an urn without consuming Them. Eleven years later, the Hosts were still perfectly intact. After careful medical and theological investigation, the fact was declared miraculous.

Cathedral where the miraculous Hosts were kept for a time

*I*n 1597, a penitent thief went to confession at the Jesuit church in Alcalá. He said he had been part of a band of Moorish marauders from the nearby mountains who had sacked numerous churches and stolen monstrances and other sacred objects in various towns, committing many sacrileges. The penitent brought with him some consecrated Hosts, which he handed over to the confessor with many tears. The confessor, very moved, immediately went to his superior to inform him. Initially it was agreed that they would consume the Hosts during a Mass; but later, fearing that the Hosts might have been poisoned as had recently happened in Murcia and Segovia, they decided to keep the Hosts in a silver casket and allow Them to decompose naturally.

Eleven years later the 24 Hosts were found still intact. The ascetic Fr. Luis de la Palma, in his capacity as Provincial, ordered that the Hosts be placed in an underground cellar along with some unconsecrated hosts. A few months later, the *unconsecrated* hosts had decomposed from the humidity, while the *consecrated* Hosts had remained intact. Six years later, Fr. de

Painting depicting a solemn procession in honor of the miraculous Hosts

Interior of the Jesuit church

Jesuit church to which the Hosts were brought back

la Palma decided to make public the miracle of the Hosts that were still intact. New academic and medical tests were carried out by His Majesty's personal physician, Garcia Carrera, as well as by numerous illustrious theologians, all of whom considered this a true miracle.

In 1619 ecclesiastical authorities officially authorized devotion to the miracle. The Sacred Hosts were publicly adored by King Phillip III, who in 1620 presided over a solemn procession in which the whole royal family participated. When Charles III later expelled the Jesuits from Spain, the Hosts were moved to the magisterial church. In 1936, when the Communist revolutionaries burned the church, the priests managed to hide the miraculous Hosts just prior to being murdered. However, to this day the Hosts have not been found. There have been many searches in the church and in the crypt, all to no avail. As yet no one has come forward with any news of the whereabouts of the 24 Hosts. "God has performed a new miracle!" exclaimed the wise historian of the city, Fr. Anselmo Raymundo Tornero, who meticulously transmitted this story to us in his work.

In Alcoy, in the year 1568, some stolen consecrated Hosts were miraculously found. The inhabitants of Alcoy celebrate the miracle each year with a festival held on the feast of Corpus Christi. The house of the man who committed the sacrilege was transformed into an oratory which can still be visited today.

On the 29th of January, 1568, a citizen of Alcoy by the name of Juan Prats, a man of French origin who needed money, furtively entered the parish church and stole many sacred objects, among which was a precious silver box containing three consecrated Hosts. Juan Prats consumed the three Hosts immediately and then hid the box in his stable underneath a pile of wood.

The next day, the parish priest, Fr. Antonio, noticed the sacrilegious theft. Distressed, he sounded the church bells to let the people know of the horrendous act. Soon all the people of Alcoy were assembled in prayer in front of the church. The search began immediately, but was in vain.

Near Juan Prat's house lived a pious widow, María Miralles, who had a statue of the Child Jesus. The woman, profoundly disturbed by the profanation of the Eucharist, began to pray intently in front of the statue of Jesus, pleading for the consecrated Hosts to be returned to the citizens of Alcoy.

Just a few hours later, María saw the little hand of the statue of Jesus point

View of Alcoy

its finger to the house of her neighbor, Juan Prats. Suspicious, she decided to tell the civil authorities. At that moment the pastor, moved by a mysterious force, went to the garden of Juan Prats' house and entered the stable. He rummaged through the pile of wood and immediately found the silver box with the three consecrated Hosts. Juan Prats, not understanding how the three Hosts he had consumed could be inside the silver box again, deeply repented and confessed his sin. The documents relating to the miracle, along with the statue of Baby Jesus, are still kept today at the Monastery of the Holy Sepulcher in Alcoy.

He rummaged through the pile of wood and immediately found the silver box with the three consecrated Hosts.

Facade of the Monastery of the Holy Sepulcher where the relics of the miracle are kept

Altar where the miraculous statue of the Child Jesus is kept

Statue of the Child Jesus which pointed to the place where the Sacred Hosts, stolen by Juan Prats, could be found

Dance of the Paloteig which takes place during the procession of the *Jesuset del Miracle*

Procession in honor of the miracle

During a Mass in Caravaca de la Cruz, Jesus appeared inside a Host together with a crucifix. Thanks to this apparition, the Muslim king of Murcia and his family were converted to Catholicism. The most authoritative document describing the miracle is the contemporary testimony of Franciscan Fr. Gilles of Zamora, the historian of King St. Ferdinand.

Cross of Caravaca

*A*mong the many documents recording this miracle, the most authoritative is that of King St. Ferdinand's historian, Fr. Gilles de Zamora. We know with certainty that a Catholic priest, Fr. Gínes Pérez Chirinos de Cuenca, traveled among the Moors in the Kingdom of Murcia with the purpose of preaching the Gospel. He was immediately taken prisoner, however, and brought into the presence of the Moorish King Zeyt-Abu-Zeyt, who asked him about certain aspects of the Christian faith. The king particularly wanted to deepen his understanding of the Mass. The priest went into detail explaining the importance of the Mass, and the king, fascinated by the preaching of the priest, ordered him to celebrate a Mass on the spot. Since the priest

did not have what was necessary for the celebration, the king ordered some of his men to get them from the nearby country of Cuenca, in Christian territory. But the cross which must be present on the altar during a Mass was forgotten. The priest began to celebrate the Mass but, at a certain point, realized that there was no cross. He became troubled and stopped.

The king asked him why he was so disturbed, and the priest told him that he needed a cross. The king however, immediately responded, "Wouldn't that be it?" In fact, at that moment two angels were placing a cross upon the altar. The priest was deeply moved and gave thanks to the Lord. He then continued the celebration with joy.

Fresco in the church

Church of Santa Cruz built where the miracle took place

Banner depicting the Cross of Caravaca

Paintings depicting the miracle

The miracle continued. At the Consecration, in place of the Host the Muslim king saw a beautiful Baby Who gazed on him endearingly. After having witnessed this miraculous event, the king and his family converted to Christianity and were baptized. Zeyt-Abu-Zeyt took the name of Vincent, and his wife took the name Elena. Since that day, the 3rd of March 1231, the place has been called *Caravaca de la Cruz*. Recently, in the Jubilee Year, the Holy See granted Caravaca de la Cruz the honor of being the fifth city in the world, along with Santiago de Compostela, St. Toribius of Liebana, Rome and Jerusalem, to celebrate the Perpetual Jubilee (every seventh year is a holy year *in perpetuum*) at the shrine where the Holy Cross is kept.

Interior of the Church of Santa Cruz

In the year 1370, during his Mass, the pastor of Cimballa was assaulted by strong doubts about the Real Presence of Jesus in the Eucharist. The Host was transformed into Flesh, and Blood began to flow copiously from the Host onto the altar linens. The episode strengthened the wavering faith of the priest, who contritely retired to a monastery, dedicating himself to a life of penance and prayer. Every year on the 12th of September, the memory of the miracle is celebrated in the parish church where the relic of the Blood-stained corporal is still kept.

Portion of the Blood-stained corporal

The "Most Holy Doubtful Mystery" is what they call the Eucharistic miracle which took place in Cimballa in 1370 in the Church of Our Lady's Purification. For months the church's pastor, Fr. Tommaso, had been plagued by doubts concerning the Real Presence of Christ in the sacrament of the Eucharist. During the celebration of Sunday Mass, after having pronounced the words of consecration, Fr. Tommaso saw Blood flowing from the Host which had been transformed into Flesh, so much that the altar linens were stained.

The penitent priest began to weep with remorse. The faithful, seeing that he was troubled, quickly hastened to the altar and saw the miracle. The relic was then taken in procession and the news spread everywhere. There were many miracles attributed to the "Most Holy Doubtful Mystery," and since then it has always been an object of great devotion on the part of the faithful. The relic of the altar linen stained with the Precious Blood has been exposed on the 12th of September every year, the anniversary of the miracle.

Large relic of the Blood-soaked corporal

The reliquary made in 1553 to contain the miraculous corporal

Church of Santa Maria in Cimballa

Panorama of Cimballa

Interior of the church

The Eucharistic miracle of Daroca took place shortly before one of the numerous battles waged by Spain against the Moors. The Christian commanders asked their chaplain to celebrate Mass, but a few minutes after the Consecration, a sudden enemy attack obliged the priest to suspend the Mass and hide the consecrated Hosts amid the sacred linens of the celebration. The Spanish were victorious, and the commanders asked the priest to give them Communion using the previously-consecrated Hosts. However, the Hosts were found completely covered with Blood. Even today, one can venerate the Blood-stained linens.

Sagrados Corporales
DAROCA

Relic of one of the two Blood-stained corporals preserved in the church in Daroca

*I*n 1239, the Christian cities of Daroca, Teruel and Calatayud (in Aragon) joined forces to take the castle of Chio Luchente back from the Moors. Before the battle, the chaplain, Fr. Mateo Martínez from Daroca, celebrated Holy Mass, during which he consecrated six Hosts intended as Communion for the six captains who led the troops: Don Jiménez Pérez, Don Fernando Sánchez, Don Pedro, Don Raimundo, Don Guillermo and Don Simone Carroz. A sudden enemy attack obliged the chaplain to immediately stop the Mass, roll the six consecrated Hosts into the corporal and hide them under a rock.

The enemy troops were forced back, and the commanders begged the priest to permit them to receive Holy Communion in thanksgiving for their victory. Fr. Mateo went to the place where he had hidden the corporal and found the Hosts drenched in Blood.

The commanders interpreted this event as a great sign of God's predilection and favor. They received Communion and tied the Blood-stained corporal to a spear, making a banner. They brought this banner into battle against the Moors and reconquered the castle of Chio, obtaining a resounding victory.

Sixteenth-century depiction of the miracle

The document describing the miracle, preserved at the collegiate church

Panoramic view of the church in Daroca

The *Santa Hijuela* (Pall) is one of the corporals of the miracle and is preserved in Carboneras

Frescos in the Chapel of Santa Hijuela, Carboneras

This triumph was attributed to the Eucharistic miracle. The six commanders each came from a different region of Spain, and each of them began to insist that the corporal go to his own city. This began a heated argument. Three times, the city of Daroca was chosen to be the custodial place of the miracle. Finally they decided to compromise. They placed the corporal on the back of a mule which would be left to wander about freely. The city where the mule would stop would be the place chosen by the Divine Will to be custodian of the corporal. The mule traveled for 12 days, walking about 200 miles, until it was exhausted. It collapsed in front of St. Mark's Church in Daroca. Afterwards, a church dedicated to Our Lady was constructed where it is still possible today to venerate the Blood-stained corporal.

Fr. Mateo went to the place where he had hidden the corporal and found the Hosts drenched in Blood.

Main altar of the church in Daroca

Chapel where the *Santa Hijuela* (Pall) is preserved, Carboneras

Paintings of the miracle in the Chapel of *Los Corporales*

Old prints depicting the miracle

Chapel of *Los Corporales*

Santa Maria Basilica, Daroca

Interior of the church

Procession held every year in honor of the Miracle of Daroca

In the town of Gerona, a priest who was celebrating Mass doubted the Real Presence of Christ in the Eucharist. But when the time for Communion arrived, he could not swallow the Host, which had changed into Flesh in his mouth. Unfortunately, the relic of the Host transformed into Flesh was destroyed in 1936 during the Spanish Civil War.

*T*his miracle took place in the church of the ancient Benedictine Monastery of St. Daniel where, until the past century, a precious reliquary was preserved containing a cloth spotted with Blood, which the people called the *Sant Dubt,* or the "Holy Doubt." In 1297, while they assisted at Mass in their chapel, the nuns noticed that at the moment of consuming the consecrated Host, the celebrant was having difficulty and seemed bewildered. A nun who was watching from the choir loft saw the priest remove something from his mouth and wrap it in the corporal, placing it on the corner of the altar.

After Mass, the nun immediately went to the altar to see what the priest had hidden in the white cloth, and with great amazement discovered that it contained a small piece of Flesh, dripping with Blood. Questioned, the priest confessed to doubting the Real Presence of Jesus in the Eucharist. Just as he had put the Sacred Host into his mouth, Its size had increased to such a volume and consistency that he was not able to swallow the Sacred Species. This is why he had wrapped the Eucharist in one of the corporals and left the Sacrament on the altar.

The monstrance which contained the Blood-stained corporal, Cathedral Museum of Gerona

Cathedral in Gerona

The Host which was changed into Flesh was then placed in a reliquary. Unfortunately, many of the documents relevant to the miracle were lost. The reliquary containing the Host-turned-into-Flesh and the Blood-soaked corporal were destroyed during the Spanish Civil War of 1936.

During the celebration of the Mass, a priest saw numerous drops of Blood falling from the consecrated Host. The miracle contributed to strengthening the faith of the priest and many of the faithful, among whom were also the royal family of Castille. There are numerous documents testifying to the miracle. The relics of the marvel were exhibited for the veneration of the faithful during the Eucharistic Congress of Toledo in 1926 and even today are the objects of deep devotion to the Spanish people as a whole.

Francisco de Zurbaran's painting of the miracle

Today at the sanctuary of Guadalupe, near Toledo, one can see the precious relics of the corporal and of the Bloodied pall (the pall is the small square of rigid linen cloth which covers the chalice and the paten) used during the miraculous Mass of the Venerable Fr. Pedro Cabañuelas. This priest was always distinguished for his deep devotion to the Holy Eucharist, and spent many hours in adoration, both night and day, before the Blessed Sacrament. Despite this, God allowed him to be severely tempted to doubt the reality of transubstantiation.

One day in the fall of 1420, during the Consecration of the Mass, he saw a dense cloud come down from above and settle above the altar. He could no longer see. Then the priest began to implore the Lord to remove his doubts. Slowly the cloud began to dissipate and a vision appeared: the Host was suspended above the chalice and numerous drops of Blood began to fall which immediately filled the chalice and overflowed onto the corporal and pall. At that point, the priest heard a voice saying: "Finish the Holy Mass, and for the present, reveal to no one what you saw."

View of Guadalupe

Retablo in the church

Church of Nuestra Señora de Guadalupe

Relic of the Blood-stained corporal

The miracle was later published by Fr. Pedro's religious brothers, and the news spread all over Spain until it reached the king of Castille, Don Juan II, and the queen, Maria of Aragon, who became so devoted to the miracle that they asked to be buried near the body of the Venerable Fr. Pedro Cabañuelas.

The parish priest of this town had strong doubts about the Real Presence of Christ in the Eucharist. One day in the year 1010, while he was celebrating Mass, a miracle occurred: the wine in the chalice was completely changed into live Blood. At present, the sacred relics are preserved in a Gothic reliquary dating back to 1426 which contains the altar cloth spotted with Blood and other relics given by Pope Sergius IV to St. Ermengol.

*H*eretical doctrines denying the Real Presence of Jesus in the Eucharist began to spread throughout all of Europe in the eleventh century. The parish priest, Fr. Bernat Oliver, also doubted the reality of transubstantiation. While he was celebrating Mass, a miracle suddenly occurred: the wine in the chalice was converted into Blood and poured onto the altar cloth, spilling onto the floor.

The Bishop of Urgell, St. Ermengol, informed of what had happened, immediately traveled to Ivorra to confirm the facts in person. These were then reported directly to Pope Sergius IV in Rome. The latter signed a papal bull which certified that a true miracle had occurred. The relics of the miracle and the pontifical document were placed under the high altar in the parish church of Ivorra, which was dedicated to St. Cugat and inaugurated in the year 1055 by Bishop William of Urgell.

Today the sacred relics are preserved in a Gothic reliquary dating back to 1426 which contains the altar cloth stained with Blood and other relics given by Pope Sergius IV to St. Ermengol.

Monstrance containing the relics of the Miracle

Detail of one of the paintings in the sanctuary depicting the changing of the wine into Blood

The sanctuary

In 1663, in order to meet the needs of the great number of pilgrims who went to venerate the miracle every year, the present sanctuary was built. Even today, each year on the second Sunday of Easter, an important feast is celebrated, known by the name *La Santa Duda* in reference to the "doubt" of Fr. Bernat Oliver, the pastor of Ivorra, and the great miracle.

The wine in the chalice changed into Blood, and the Precious Blood poured onto the altar cloth and spilled onto the floor.

Sanctuary where the miracle occured

Relic of the Blood-stained corporal

Church of El Cugat where the relics of the miracle are kept

Interior of the Church of St. Cugat

Detail of the monstrance containing the sacred relics

The Eucharistic Miracle of
MONCADA

SPAIN, 1392

At the end of the 14th century, the French Cardinals had elected an anti-pope, hoping that he would transfer the Holy See back to Avignon. This event created great confusion among the clergy, to the point that many priests started to doubt whether they had been validly ordained. In the Eucharistic miracle of Moncada, Baby Jesus appeared in the Host to dissipate the doubts of a priest uncertain about the validity of his priestly ordination. Fr. Odorico Raynaldi described this miracle in his *Anales Eclesiásticos*. The story is also narrated in numerous other documents kept in the archives of the city of Moncada.

La V. Virgen Inès de Moncada.

Inés lived her whole life as a hermit and penitent in the cave known as *El Rodeno*, which is still a pilgrimage site today

The election of Pope Urban VI (April 18, 1378) was strongly opposed by the French Cardinals, who wanted a French Pope in the hopes that he would transfer the Holy See back to Avignon. On September 20, 1378, they elected the anti-pope Clement VII. The schismatics immediately tried to seize Rome by force of arms, but their attempts failed. Therefore they retreated to Avignon, where Clement VII continued to act as if he were the legitimate pontiff.

During this period of great uncertainty, Fr. Mosén Jaime Carrós, a priest in Moncada, was living in anguish, thinking that his ordination was inval-

id since a Bishop appointed by the anti-pope Clement VII had ordained him. Every time he celebrated Mass he greatly feared he was deceiving the faithful by distributing unconsecrated hosts. He was also terrified that none of the other sacraments he was performing were valid. The priest ardently prayed for the Lord to give him some sign of confirmation. He received an answer on Christmas Day 1392.

That day, a woman named Angela Alpicat attended Mass with her five-year-old daughter, Inés (the future St. Inés de Moncada). At the end of Mass, the little girl refused to leave

The Janua Coeli Monastery in the valley of Lullén, ancient property of Inés' family, later on given to the monks

Inés in the cave where she lived as a hermit

Representation of the miracle

The church where the miracle took place

the church, imploring her mother to let her remain there to play with the beautiful Child the pastor had held in his arms during the Consecration.

On December 26, Lady Angela went to Mass again, and when the priest lifted the Host, the little girl again saw the Child in the hands of the priest. At the end of Mass, Lady Angela told the priest about her daughter's visions. Fr. Carrós immediately examined the girl. Little Inés answered all the priest's questions without any difficulty. The priest, however, wanted to test her further and invited her to attend Mass on the following day. That day, he took two hosts, but he consecrated only one of them. Then, taking the *consecrated* Host, the priest asked the little girl what she could see in his hands. She answered, "I see Baby Jesus." Then he lifted the *unconsecrated* host and asked the same question. "I see a little white disk," Inés answered. The priest was overwhelmed with joy, and the whole congregation exulted in seeing the validity of their pastor's ordination confirmed. Although an anti-pope had ordained the Bishop who ordained Moncada's pastor, Fr. Carrós, God had remained faithful to the apostolic succession determined by the imposition of the Bishop's hands.

The Eucharistic miracle of Montserrat leads us to reflect on the reality of Purgatory and reminds us that every Mass has infinite value because it makes present the one sacrifice of Christ suffering on Calvary. This Eucharistic miracle is reported by the Benedictine priest Fr. Francio de Paula Crusellas in his book *Nueva historia del Santuario y Monasterio de Nuestra Señora de Montserrat.*

Interior of the church where the miracle took place

*I*n 1657, Fr. Bernardo de Ontevieros, Father General of the Benedictine Order in Spain, and Abbot Millán de Mirando were at the Monastery of Our Lady of Montserrat to attend some conferences. During one of the conferences, a woman and her young daughter showed up at the monastery. The daughter began to beg Abbot Millán to celebrate three Masses for her deceased father, wholeheartedly convinced that by these Masses the soul of her father would be freed from the pains of Purgatory. The good abbot, moved by the girl's tears, celebrated the first Mass of suffrage the next day,

and the girl, who was present with her mother, said she saw her father kneeling, surrounded by frightening flames, on the step of the main altar during the Consecration. The Father General, in order to find out whether her story was true, dubiously asked the girl to put a handkerchief close to the flames that surrounded her father. At his request, the girl put the handkerchief into the fire, which only she could see. Immediately all the monks saw the handkerchief burst into flame.

During the second Mass, the girl said she saw her father dressed in a brightly-

The miraculous Madonna of Montserrat

Sanctuary of Our Lady of Montserrat

colored robe standing next to the deacon. At the third and last Mass, the father appeared to his daughter dressed in a snow-white robe. As soon as the Mass ended the girl exclaimed, "There is my father going away and rising up to Heaven!" The girl then thanked the community of monks on behalf of her father, as he had asked her to do. The Father General of the Benedictine Order in Spain, the Bishop of Astorga, and numerous citizens of the town were present.

In the Eucharistic miracle of O'Cebreiro, during Mass, the Host changed into Flesh and the wine changed into Blood which gushed out of the chalice, staining the corporal. The Lord worked this marvel to sustain the weak faith of the priest, who did not believe in the Real Presence of Jesus in the Eucharist. To this day, the relics of the miracle are kept in the church where the prodigy took place, and numerous pilgrims go there annually to venerate them.

Relics of the chalice, paten and Precious Blood of the miracle

One icy winter day in 1300, a Benedictine priest was celebrating Mass in a side chapel of the convent church of O'Cebreiro. On that miserable day of endless snow and unbearably freezing wind, he thought no one would show up for Mass. He was wrong. A farmer from Barxamaior by the name of Juan Santín climbed up to the convent to attend Mass. The priest saying the Mass, who did not believe in the Real Presence of Christ in the Most Holy Eucharist, interiorly despised the farmer's sacrifice and good will. He began to celebrate the Mass. Immediately after having pronounced the words of consecration, the Host changed to Flesh and the wine changed to Blood, gushing out of the chalice and staining the corporal. At that moment, it seems, even the head of the wooden statue of Our Lady bowed in adoration. The people today call her the "Madonna of the Holy Miracle." The Lord wanted to open the eyes of the unbelieving priest who had doubted and to reward the farmer for his great devotion.

For almost two hundred years the Host-changed-to-Flesh was left on the paten until Queen Isabella learned about

Mountain where Juan Santín used to retreat and pray

Sanctuary of O'Cebreiro

Altar where the miracle took place

The Madonna of the miracle

Panoramic view of O'Cebreiro

Panoramic view from the Monastery of O'Cebreiro

Chapel where the relics of the miracle are kept

Interior of Santa Maria Church

the miracle as she was passing through O'Cebreiro on pilgrimage to Santiago de Compostela. The queen immediately had a precious crystal shrine custommade to hold the miraculous Host. Every year on the feast of Corpus Christi, on August 15th, and on September 8th, the relics are taken in procession along with the statue of Our Lady. Among the many documents testifying to the miracle are the 1487 bull of Pope Innocent VIII, that of Pope Alexander VII of 1496, and an account by Fr. Yepes.

A monstrance containing a consecrated Host was stolen from the parish church in Onil. Days later, a woman from the nearby town of Tibi found the stolen monstrance, with the consecrated Host inside, in a grassy field. Exactly 119 years later, on November 28, 1943, Fr. Guillermo Hijarrubia, delegate of the Archbishop of Valencia, confirmed the authenticity of the miracle, noting the perfect preservation of the Host. To this day the consecrated Host has remained intact in spite of the nearly 200 years which have elapsed.

The still-intact Host

*O*n November 15, 1824, Nicolás Bernabeu, who had been an altar boy in the church of Onil from the time he was little, stole the monstrance containing the Blessed Sacrament, along with some other sacred objects, from the church. News of the sacrilegious theft spread so quickly throughout the region that when the thief tried to sell the stolen objects in Alicante, he aroused the suspicions of the dealer, who notified the authorities. Nicolás Bernabeu was arrested, but did not want to reveal where he had hidden the monstrance, which still contained the Blessed Sacrament. The faithful and the civil authorities looked for days all over the countryside. However, in the nearby town of Tibi, where the thief lived, a woman named Teresa Carbonell found the stolen monstrance on November 28, 1824, in the area called *La Pedredia*. Immediately the woman returned the Blessed Sacrament to Onil, where she was received with great rejoicing.

Exactly 119 years later, on November 28, 1943, Fr. Guillermo Hijarrubia, delegate of the Archbishop of Valencia, confirmed the authenticity of the miracle, verifying the perfect preservation of the Host contained in the stolen monstrance.

Shrine of the miraculous Host

Festival called *La Pedredia* in memory of the finding of the Host

To this day, in St. James the Apostle Church in Onil, one can adore the miraculous Host which is still intact after almost two centuries. Every year the Feast of Our Lord "Robat" is celebrated in memory of this Eucharistic miracle and the finding of the Host.

Immediately the woman brought the Host back to Onil, where she was received with great jubilation.

ADORADO SEA EL SANTISIMO SACRAMENTO
AVE MARIA PURISIMA

Sagrada Hostia incorrupta
venerada en Onil desde el año 1824

Adoración Nocturna Española
DIOCESIS DE ORIHUELA - ALICANTE
SOLEMNE VIGILIA DIOCESANA DE ESPIGAS
Y CONMEMORACION DE BODAS DE ORO
(SECCION DE ONIL)
1.941 - 1.991

❋

ONIL (Alicante)
6 de Julio de 1.991

Interior of St. James Church

Chapel constructed on the site where the Hosts were found

Scenes from the miracle in the stained glass windows of St. James Church

In the miracle of Ponferrada, Juan de Benavente decided to steal from his own parish, the tabernacle which contained a precious silver ciborium holding numerous consecrated Hosts. Only long afterwards, in miraculous circumstances, were the stolen Hosts found. They were still perfectly preserved.

Painting of the miracle, currently housed in the new St. Peter's Church

Juan de Benavente lived in Ponferrada with his wife. Seemingly, he was very devout and religious; in fact, every evening he stopped in church to pray. One day during his prayer time, he succumbed to greed and seized the tabernacle, a simple wooden container, in which there was a precious silver ciborium containing some consecrated Hosts. He fled from the church and headed towards the Sil River to pitch the cheap wooden tabernacle, but when he tried to throw it into the water, he could not do so because it had become extremely heavy. So he returned home where he hid everything, saying nothing to his wife.

During the night, however, continuous flashes of light came from the tabernacle, arousing the suspicions of his wife. So Juan decided to go out and definitively dispose of his sacrilegiously stolen goods. He reached a place the townspeople called the "Arenal Field" and threw the tabernacle and consecrated Hosts into some brambles.

The discovery of the crime dismayed the whole population, and Juan became increasingly nervous and anxious, partly because he did not know how to sell the silver ciborium without getting caught.

The old St. Peter's Church, demolished in the 20th century, where the painting of the miracle was previously housed, Ponferrada

The Virgin of the Evergreen Oak

St. Mary's Church where the miracle took place, Ponferrada

Sil River, near the Arenal Field, where Juan de Benavente wanted to throw the tabernacle containing the Hosts

Street named in honor of the miracle

New St. Peter's Church, Ponferrada

Exact spot where the Hosts were found

Near the Arenal Field, the owner of the land, Diego Nuñez de Losada, set up a target practice for entertainment during a local festival. The Hosts were still in the brambles, and eyewitnesses reported seeing flashes of light at night and strange doves hovering there during the day. The archers tried in vain to hit the doves. The miller, a Mr. Nogaledo, then decided to capture the doves with his own hands and ventured into the bushes, discovering the tabernacle and the Hosts from which intense flashes of light emanated. In a state of shock, he ran to the church and began to ring the bells.

The return of the Hosts to the church was immediately organized with a solemn procession. Juan was overcome with remorse and decided to confess his guilt. On the spot where the miraculous Hosts were found, a chapel was immediately constructed. In 1570 the parish priest enlarged the building and, in memory of the miracle, instituted a solemn annual procession on the octave of Corpus Christi.

In 887, Count Vifred founded a monastery in the Pyrenese region of Catalonia, around which a village soon developed. Today this village is called "San Juan de las Abadesas." Here a crucifix is still preserved with a Host—which has remained intact since 1251—imbedded in the forehead of the figure of Jesus.

Face of the wooden statue of Jesus in which is preserved the miraculous Host

In 1251 some wood carvings were sculpted in the monastery church of San Juan de las Abadesas, depicting the deposition of Jesus from the Cross, with the figures of Jesus and His Mother Mary, Joseph of Arimathea, Nicodemus, St. John the beloved disciple, and the two thieves. These beautiful statues, saved from destruction during the 1936 Spanish Civil War, are so expressive that they deeply move many people. Jesus' head is especially beautiful.

When the crucifix was carved, the artist made a depression in Jesus' forehead, approximately two and a half inches in diameter, with the idea of preserving the Eucharist in it. In 1251 someone put a consecrated Host there, but over time this was forgotten.

Only in 1426, while the statues were being restored, was the cavity in the forehead of the crucifix discovered, sealed by a small silver plaque. Inside, wrapped in a white linen cloth, the Host consecrated in 1251 was found totally incorrupt. Since then, that Host, known as "The Most Holy Mystery of San Juan de las Abadesas," has been adored and visited by numerous pilgrims.

Monastery of San Juan de las Abadesas

JUAN DE LAS ABADESAS 15 El Santísimo Misterio, Descendiendo EDIT. SALVADO

A consecrated Host was stolen by a Christian woman of Saragossa to make a love potion. As soon as she got home, the Child Jesus appeared in the Host. The document which describes the miracle in detail is preserved in the municipal archives of Saragossa. In the cathedral, next to the Chapel of San Dominguito del Val, there is an old painting with an inscription beside it accurately recounting the marvelous event.

Cathedral in Saragossa

*T*his Eucharistic miracle took place in the city of Saragossa in 1427, when the Bishop of the city was Alonso Arhuello. Fr. Dorner, archdeacon of the city, left a written report of the event: "A married woman consulted a Moorish evil sorcerer for a remedy to cure her husband of his violent nature and to make him treat her more gently. The sorcerer told her he needed her to bring him a consecrated Host to change the husband's behavior. This very superstitious woman went to St. Michael's Church, went to confession and received the Eucharist. With diabolical cunning, she took the Blessed Sacrament from her mouth and hid the Host in a little box which she immediately took to the sorcerer.

"When they opened the box, instead of the Host they saw, to their great terror, a little Baby surrounded by light. The sorcerer told the woman to take the box home, burn the Holy Eucharist, and bring the ashes to him. The unscrupulous woman did as she was told, but with great amazement saw that though the box was completely burned, the Baby remained unharmed.

"Stricken with terror and beside herself, she ran to the sorcerer's house to tell him what had happened. The sorcerer, on hearing the woman's words,

Main altar

Chapel of the Holy Christ

Exterior of the cathedral

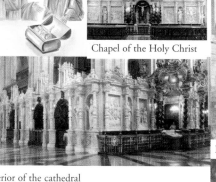

Interior of the cathedral

Painting representing the miracle, Chapel of San Dominguito del Val. There is also a marble plaque describing the miracle.

began to tremble, fearing vengeance from heaven. They decided to go to the cathedral to inform Bishop Alonso, confess their sin and ask for baptism.

"The Bishop consulted some prelates and theologians of the diocese to shed light on the matter, and it was finally decided to take the Miraculous Baby in solemn procession from the woman's house back to the cathedral. The whole city turned out into the streets to accompany the procession, and everyone was deeply moved at the sight of the marvelous Baby. Once in the cathedral, the miraculous Baby was placed on the altar in the Chapel of St. Valerius so that the people of Saragossa could see Him and venerate Him. The following day, while the Bishop was celebrating Mass at the same altar, another miracle took place: at the words of consecration, a Host, which was immediately consumed by the Bishop, appeared where the Baby was. Thanks to this Eucharistic miracle, devotion to the Blessed Sacrament was revived throughout Saragossa." This document is preserved in the town archives.

The Eucharistic miracle of Silla happened in 1907. Some Hosts, stolen by unknown thieves, were found in perfect condition, hidden under a stone in a little garden not far from the city. Today one can still adore the miraculous Hosts: they have remained intact for over 100 years. The Hosts are preserved in the Church of Our Lady of the Angels in Silla.

During Mass on March 25, 1907, the Feast of the Annunciation, Fr. Fernando Gomez, pastor of the Church of Our Lady of the Angels in Silla, went to the tabernacle to take out the Hosts for the Communion of the faithful. He was greatly perturbed to find the little tabernacle door open and the precious silver ciborium with all the consecrated Hosts missing.

The Hosts were found two days later in a small garden outside the city, hidden under a stone. The pastor formed a solemn procession to take Them back to the church.

In 1934, seeing that the Hosts remained "in the same state in which they were found under the stone and that they had maintained their original condition unchanged," the Archbishop of Valencia began a process to declare their preservation miraculous, and sealed the reliquary containing the Hosts with wax. He also wrote a detailed account of the miracle. Unfortunately, two years later the Bishop's residence was burned down by the anarchist Communists, and the precious document was lost. In 1982, Archbishop Miguel Roca, the Archbishop of Valencia, undertook a new canonical process by which he officially authorized veneration of the Hosts.

I CENTENARIO DE LAS
SAGRADAS FORMAS INCORRUPTA
SILLA. 1907 - 2007

Miraculous Hosts

Church of Our Lady of the Angels, Silla

The historical facts about the Holy Grail have often been distorted and misrepresented. This precious object has always been at the center of fanciful tales and novels like the legend of the Knights of the Round Table in England and the stories of Percival in France and Parzival in Germany during the twelfth and thirteenth centuries. This theme was also used by Wagner in a Christian-esoteric perspective, and at the end of the twentieth century, the fantasy novels of B. Cornwell favored the birth of a writing trend still alive today.

The Holy Grail of Valencia

The Holy Grail of Valencia is the chalice used by Jesus at His Last Supper with the Apostles to consecrate and offer the Eucharistic wine that is His Blood, but it has also been identified as the cup in which Joseph of Arimathea collected the Blood of Jesus at the foot of the Cross.

The Grail has many names: *San Grëal*, *Holy Grail*, *Sangreal* in England, *Sanct Graal* and *Saint Graal* in old and modern French, and *Gral* and *Graal* in German. The name comes from the Latin *gradalis* or *gratalis*, meaning "vase" or glass.

From many sources, we know that a few centuries after the death of Christ the Holy Grail was being shown to Christian pilgrims in Jerusalem. According to the account of Arculf, a French Bishop who lived in the Holy Land in 720 A.D, the chalice in which the Lord Himself consecrated His own Blood was preserved in the Church of the Holy Sepulcher in Jerusalem. The Venerable Bede adds that the cup was protected by a net and that it could be touched and kissed through an opening. No one knows exactly when the chalice was taken from Jerusalem; most probably this happened in the seventh century.

Text of the note written by Juan de Ribera in which he certifies that "till now the Holy Chalice is preserved in our cathedral"

Document regarding the reception of the Holy Grail in the Cathedral of Valencia in 1437

Route traveled by the Holy Grail

Cathedral of Valencia

John Paul II kisses the Holy Grail of Valencia

Today, in the Gothic chapel of the "Santo Caliz" ("Holy Chalice") in Valencia's cathedral, a miraculous chalice, identified by tradition as the Holy Grail, is kept and shown for the veneration of the faithful. This precious object is formed of different parts: the inverted upper part of an agate chalice constitutes the base; the stem is enriched by precious stones; and the upper part is a cup, also made of agate. These parts are attributed to different eras; the cup is the oldest and the most difficult to date and constitutes the most interesting part. On the base is found an inscription in Arabic of disputed meaning, which, however, could be another indication of the chalice's age. According to Professor Salvador Antuñano, "When we know the mystery of the Chalice of the Holy Grail, we realize that there is nothing enigmatic or esoteric about it. The history of this precious chalice concerns the most dramatic, most sublime event ever to happen to humanity: the history of the Word made Man and Eucharist."

The Holy Grail of Valencia is the chalice used by Jesus at His Last Supper with the Apostles to consecrate and offer the Eucharistic wine that is His Blood, but it has also been identified as the cup in which Joseph of Arimathea collected the Blood of Jesus at the foot of the Cross.

The Last Supper. Juan de Juarez, Prado Museum (Madrid)

Precious monstrance preserved in the cathedral of Valencia

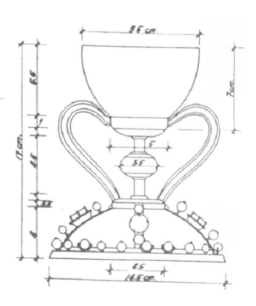

◆ Ettiswil

In Ettiswil, there is a shrine dedicated to a Eucharistic miracle that happened in 1447. Anna Vögtli, a member of a satanic sect, was able to steal a pyx containing a large Host from the parish church. The Host was found near a fence among some nettle bushes, hovering in the air and surrounded by a bright light, and was divided into seven pieces which were joined together so that they looked like a flower. Many Popes granted indulgences to the shrine's visitors. The great feast of the miracle takes place on Laetare Sunday and on the two following days.

Painting portraying the Miracle of Ettiswil, Hiéron Museum, Paray-le-Monial

*T*he most important document describing this miracle is the *Protocol of Justice*. This was compiled on July 16, 1447, by Hermann von Rüsseg, Lord of Buron. The translation reads: "On Wednesday, May 23, 1447, the Blessed Sacrament was stolen from the parish church in Ettiswil, and was found soon afterwards by Margaret Schulmeister, a young swineherd. The Holy Eucharist was not far from the parish church, close to a fence and thrown on the ground among nettles; It looked like a bright flower."

After investigation, the police arrested a young woman, Anna Vögtli from Bischoffingen, who of her own accord immediately confessed everything: "Having slipped my hand into the narrow iron grate, I got hold of the large Host. But as soon as I went beyond the cemetery wall, the Host became so heavy that I was unable to carry It any further. Unable to go either forwards or backwards, I threw the Host into some nettles close to a hedge."

The Host was found by Mrs. Margaret Schulmeister, who had a herd of pigs,

Interior of the shrine

Altarpiece on which scenes of the miracle are portrayed

Detail of the altarpiece in which scenes from miracle are portrayed

Relic of the miracle

Shrine at Ettiswil

and she stated that "once I arrived with my pigs close to where the Blessed Sacrament had been thrown, my animals did not want to go further. I asked the help of two men who were passing by on horseback. In the grass the two men saw the stolen Host divided into seven sections. Six of the sections formed a flower similar to a rose, with a great light surrounding them."

The local parish priest was informed. At once, together with all his parishioners, he went to pick up the Host and bring It back to the church. He picked up the six sections, but when he tried to pick up the main central section, it disappeared into the ground before the eyes of all. This disappearance was interpreted as a sign, and it was decided to build a chapel precisely at the spot where the Host had disappeared. The six sections were kept in the church of Ettiswil and became the object of great veneration by the inhabitants of the village and by foreigners. God performed many miracles there. The chapel and the altar were consecrated on December 28, 1448, a year and a half after the events.

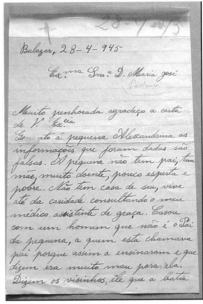

Alexandrina was paralyzed at age 21 because of a dramatic incident in which she fled from the threat of violence. She did not permit herself to be overcome by sadness and loneliness, but thought: "Jesus, You are a prisoner in the tabernacle as I am here in my bed, so we can keep each other company." In addition to the physical sufferings from her paralysis, she also endured mystical sufferings: for four years, she suffered the pains of the Passion every Friday, and after this period, for another 13 years until her death, she was nourished by the Eucharist alone. Her life became a continuous prayer for the conversion of sinners.

A letter of Alexandrina in her own handwriting

Alexandrina Maria was born in Balasar, Portugal, on March 30, 1904. At age 14, in order to escape an attack by three men and to maintain her purity, she jumped from a window. The consequences of this were terrible, though not immediate. Several years later, she was bedridden from a progressive paralysis, from which she suffered the remaining 30 years of her life. Yet she did not despair, but entrusted herself to Jesus with these words: "As You are a prisoner in the tabernacle, and I, according to Your will, am a prisoner in my bed, we can keep each other company." She began to have ever more powerful mystical experiences, and from Friday, October 3, 1938, until March 24, 1942, she relived the sufferings of the Passion 182 times.

From 1942 until her death, Alexandrina was nourished by the Eucharist alone, and during a period of observation at Foce del Douro Hospital near Oporto, for forty days and forty nights she was under supervision by several doctors in her absolute fast and her condition of *anuria* (absence of urine). After 10 long years of paralysis which she offered as Eucharistic reparation and for the conversion of sinners, on July 30, 1935, Jesus appeared to her, saying: "I have put you in the world so that you may draw life only from Me, to bear witness to the world how precious the Eucharist is. [...] The strongest chain that keeps souls in bondage to Satan is the flesh and sins of impurity. Never has there been such a spread of vice, wickedness and crime as there is today!

Alexandrina Maria da Costa

On her tomb are the words she wished to be placed there: "Sinners, if the ashes of my body can be useful for your salvation, draw near to them, pass above them, and trample on them until they vanish. But sin no more; do not offend our Jesus any longer!"

Alexandrina relived the sorrows of Jesus' Passion every Friday

Father Emanuel Vilar, one of Alexandrina's spiritual directors

The home of Alexandrina at Balasar

The Jesuit Father Pinho guided Alexandrina in a special way, and it was thanks to him that many of her writings were submitted to the Pope

Alexandrina with her mother and sister

Alexandrina with one of her spiritual directors

Never has there been so much sin [...] The Eucharist—My Body and Blood—Behold, the Eucharist is the salvation of the world."

Mary also appeared to Alexandrina on September 12, 1949, with the Rosary in her hand, saying to her, "The world is in agony, dying in sin. I desire prayer and penance. Protect all whom you love and the whole world with this, my Rosary."

On October 13, 1955, the anniversary of the last apparition of the Blessed Mother at Fatima, Alexandrina was heard exclaiming: "I'm happy because I'm going to heaven." She died at 7:30 in the evening that very day.

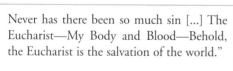

St. Nicholas von Flue, better known as "Brother Klaus," was declared the patron saint of Switzerland by Pope Pius XII in 1947. He was born into a farmer's family in 1417 in Flüeli in the Alpine foothills above Sachseln, in the region of Obwald. He married, had ten children, and led a normal life until he was 50. Then he felt a very strong call from God to leave everything and follow Him. He therefore asked for three graces: to obtain the consent of his wife Dorothy and their older children; never to feel the temptation to turn back; and finally, God willing, to be able to live without eating or drinking. All his requests were granted. He lived for twenty years in the forest as a hermit with no food except for the Eucharist, as many witnesses testified.

ANDRÉ FROSSARD

FRANCE 20TH CENTURY

The conversion of atheist writer André Frossard in the presence of the Holy Eucharist had great repercussions around the world. He himself recounted his conversion story in his book, *God Exists: I Have Met Him* (1969). Up to his final days, he kept repeating over and over: "From the time I encountered God, I have never been able to grasp the mystery of God. Every day is something new for me. And if God exists, I must speak of Him; if Christ is the Son of God, I must proclaim it loudly; if there is eternal life, I must preach it."

Hans Friers, *The Living Cross,* Fribourg

*I*n Frossard's own words: "Having entered a chapel in the Latin Quarter of Paris at 5:10 in the morning to look for a friend, I left at 5:15 in the company of a friendship that was not of this earth. Having entered as a skeptic and an atheist…in fact, beyond skeptical and atheistic, I was indifferent and preoccupied by so many things other than a God to Whom I never gave a thought, not even to deny Him… I was standing by the door, looking around for my friend, but did not find him….

"My gaze passed from the shadows to the light…from the faithful gathered there, to the nuns, to the altar…and came to rest on the second candle burning to the left of the Cross (unaware that I was standing in the presence of the Blessed Sacrament). And at that point, suddenly a series of miracles unfolded whose indescribable force shattered in an instant the absurd being that I was, to bring to birth the amazed child that I had never been…. At first these words, '*Spiritual Life*', came to me…as if they had been pronounced in a whisper next to me…then came a great light…a world, another world of a radiance and substance which in one stroke cast our world among the fragile shadows of unfulfilled dreams…the evidence of God…of Whom I felt all the sweetness…a sweetness which was active and jarring beyond any form of violence, capable of breaking the hardest stone and even what is harder than stone—the human heart.

André Frossard

"Its overflowing eruption, so complete, was accompanied by a joy which is the exultation of the saved, the joy of one shipwrecked who is rescued just in time. These sensations, which I find difficult to translate into a language which cannot capture these ideas and images, were all simultaneous.... Everything is dominated by the Presence...of Him Whose name I would never be able to write for fear of harming its tenderness, of Him before Whom I have had the good fortune to be a forgiven child who wakes up to discover that everything is a gift...."

Frossard commented: "God existed and was present, revealed, once upon a time masked until that delegation of light brought all into my comprehension and love without words or figures.... Only one thing surprised me: The Eucharist! Not that it seemed incredible, but it amazed me that Divine Charity would have chosen this silent way to communicate Himself, and above all that He would choose to become bread, which is the staple of the poor and the food preferred by children...."

Frossard ended his confession with this beautiful sentiment: "O Love, eternity will be too short to speak of You."

BL. ANNE CATHERINE EMMERICH

GERMANY, 1774-1824

Anne Catherine Emmerich was forced to leave the monastery where she lived because it was taken over by the government. At the same time, her health declined and her mystical experiences increased: she received the stigmata and had numerous visions. One of these visions made it possible to find the house of Our Lady in Ephesus. According to ancient tradition, it seems that Mary settled, together with John the Apostle, in this city. The miraculous aspect of Anne Catherine's life is that for years she lived only on the Eucharist.

House where Our Lady lived in Ephesus, found thanks to the visions of Anne Catherine

Anne Catherine Emmerich was born in Germany on September 8, 1774, into a family of farmers, and began to work at a very young age. Later on, a religious vocation matured and she asked to be admitted at several monasteries, but she was always rejected because she was very poor and had no dowry. Only when she was 28 was she accepted into the monastery of Agnetenberg, where she fervently took part in monastic life, always ready to take on the most difficult tasks.

One night while she was praying, Jesus appeared and offered her a crown of roses and a crown of thorns. She chose the crown of thorns, and Jesus placed the crown on her head. Immediately, the first stigmata appeared on her forehead. Later on, after another apparition of Jesus, wounds also appeared in her hands, feet and side.

In 1811, the monastery at Agnetenberg was suppressed. Anne Catherine found a position as housekeeper for a priest, but soon became ill and bedridden.

Dr. Wesener, a young doctor, visited her and was very impressed by the stigmata. During the next eleven years, he became her friend and faithful assistant, keeping a diary in which he transcribed her visions. Meanwhile,

Portrait of Clemens Brentano

Portrait of Anne Catherine Emmerich

Sketch by Clemens Brentano

House where Catherine was born

the nun had practically stopped eating: a little water and the consecrated Host were enough to keep her alive for years. She was very devoted to, and wrote many pages about, the Holy Eucharist: "My desire for the Holy Eucharist was so vehement and irresistible that, at night, I would often leave my cell to go to the church... Often I would genuflect and prostrate towards the Blessed Sacrament with arms extended, and sometimes I would go into ecstasy." Anne Catherine always united her sufferings with those of Jesus and offered them for the redemption of mankind.

The most famous biographer of Anne Catherine was the German writer Clemens von Brentano, who wrote down all her visions. Brentano compiled thousands of pages about the Blessed, many of which are still unpublished. In one of his most famous passages he wrote: "Anne Catherine stands like a street sign indicating the right direction to the faithful. What she says is brief but simple, full of depth, warmth and life. I understood everything. Always happy, affectionate, dignified, marvelous; always ill, agonizing, but at the same time delicate and fresh, chaste, tried, lucid. To be seated at her side meant to occupy the most beautiful place in the world."

ST. BERNARD OF CLAIRVAUX

FRANCE, 12TH CENTURY

St. Bernard was the central character in an important Eucharistic miracle. The Duke of Aquitaine had separated himself from the Catholic Church and had absolutely no intention of returning. After celebrating Mass, St. Bernard went before the duke and presented the Blessed Sacrament to him. The duke, deeply moved by a mysterious force, fell to his knees, begging forgiveness for having left the Catholic Church.

A 17th-century Baroque painting, *William of Aquitaine Converted by St. Bernard*. Photo courtesy of *The Record*, taken by Marnie McAllister.

One of Saint Bernard's biographers recounts that the saint "came to Aquitaine to reconcile to the Church the duke of this province, but since the latter refused to be reconciled, the saint of God went to the altar to celebrate Mass, while the duke, who had been excommunicated, waited for him outside the church door.

"After the Consecration, Bernard placed the Host on the paten and exited the church, his face aflame with holy anger. When he reached the duke, he admonished him with these words: 'We pleaded with you, and you ridiculed us. Now He, the Son of the Virgin, the Lord of the Church, He Whom you persecute, has come to you. Behold, you have here before you the Judge in whose hands you will one day find your soul. Do you dare reject Him as you have rejected His servant? Resist Him if you can.'

"The duke immediately felt his legs buckle beneath him and prostrated himself at the feet of Bernard, who then ordered him to stand up to hear God's sentence. The duke stood up, trembling, and carried out all that Bernard ordered him to do."

ST. JOHN BOSCO

St. John Bosco was always very devoted to the Eucharist. In numerous writings the saint speaks of the importance of this Sacrament. Once, when there were only eight Hosts left in the ciborium, he began to multiply them so that he was able to distribute Communion to 360 youth who were present at Mass!

*B*iographers recount that in 1848, during one of his Masses, Don Bosco realized just as he was about to distribute Communion to 360 young people that the ciborium in the tabernacle contained only eight Hosts. Everyone noticed and wondered what Don Bosco would do. Joseph Buzzetti, who later became one of the first Salesian priests, was serving Mass that day. When he saw Don Bosco multiply the Hosts and give Communion to the 360 boys, he was overcome with emotion.

Don Bosco relates that he saw in a dream a terrible sea battle caused by a multitude of boats, both large and small, fighting against a single majestic ship, a symbol of the Church. Struck many times but always victorious, the ship was guided by the Pope to anchor securely between two tall pillars in the sea. The first held up a huge Host with the inscription, "Salvation of the Faithful," and the other pillar, which was lower, supported a statue of Mary Immaculate with the inscription, "Help of Christians."

Jesus appeared to St. Catherine of Siena to reveal to her that just as a great flame neither diminishes nor goes out even if used to light many candles, so the great fire of the Holy Eucharist loses nothing as It inflames the faithful who come with their weak or strong faith. The weakness or strength of each one's faith was symbolized by different sizes of candles.

St. Catherine of Siena sees fire issuing from the consecrated Host. Diocesan Museum of Milan

Regarding the Eucharist, Jesus confided the following to St. Catherine of Siena: "You receive the whole divine essence in that sweetest Sacrament under the whiteness of the bread. Just as the sun cannot be divided, so the God-Man cannot be divided in the whiteness of the Host. Let us suppose that the Sacred Host is broken: even if it were possible to break It into thousands of tiny Particles, Christ, fully God and fully Man, is in every one of them. In the same manner as a mirror shatters into thousands of pieces, but does not shatter the image you see in it, so if the Host is broken, the image of the God-Man is not broken; the whole God-Man is present in each part. And He is not diminished, just as with fire: If you had one candle and everyone in the whole world came to light his candle from that single candle, the flame would not diminish, and each one would have an entire flame. It is true that some would receive more or less of the candle's light, because everyone would receive exactly the amount of fire he needs to light the material he brings.

"To help you understand better, I will give you another example. If there

Often St. Catherine saw a baby instead of a Host in the hand of the priest; at other times she saw a burning furnace which the priest seemed to enter at the time of Holy Communion. From the Hiéron Museum at Paray-le-Monial.

were many people bringing candles of all sizes—one person with a one-ounce candle and others with candles weighing two or six ounces, one with a one-pound candle and others having larger candles—and if they all went to light their candles from the one, it is true that in each lit candle, no matter how large or small it is, one would be able to see the whole flame—its warmth, color and light. Nevertheless you would say that he who has a one-ounce candle has less light than the one with a one-pound candle. Thus it is for those who receive this Sacrament. The soul brings its candle, which is holy desire, to receive this Sacrament, but this candle by itself is unlit and is ignited by the reception of the Eucharist. In fact, although all of you have the same material, because all of you are created in My image and likeness, and as Christians all have the light of baptism, yet each one can grow in love and virtue, as much as you like, through My grace. You do not change the supernatural life I have given you, but you can grow and increase in the love of virtue, using your free will, with virtue and charitable affection while you still have time—because once time has passed, this will no longer be possible."

ST. CLARE OF ASSISI

ITALY, 1240

The History of Saint Clare, Virgin tells of various miracles performed by St. Clare. There are accounts of multiplication of loaves and bottles of oil appearing in the convent where there was nothing before. But Clare performed the most famous of her miracles in 1240, on a Friday in September, when, by showing them the Sacred Host, she turned away an attack by Saracen soldiers who had broken into the convent cloister.

Icon in the Basilica of St. Clare of Assisi. Clare's faith in the Son of God and of Mary, hidden in the poverty of the Eucharistic Bread, destroyed the strength of her enemies

This Eucharistic miracle is cited in *The History of Saint Clare, Virgin,* written by Tommaso da Celano, and describes how St. Clare of Assisi succeeded, with the help of the Blessed Sacrament, in turning away Saracen troops in the pay of Emperor Frederick II of Swabia.

The *History* recounts the story thus: "By imperial order, regiments of Saracen soldiers and bowmen were stationed there (near Assisi), massed like bees, ready to devastate the encampments and seize the cities. Once, during an enemy attack against Assisi, city beloved of the Lord, and while the army was already approaching the gates, the fierce Saracens invaded San Damiano, entered the confines of the monastery and even the very cloister of the virgins. The women swooned in terror, their voices trembling with fear as they cried out to their mother, St. Clare.

"St. Clare, with a fearless heart, commanded them to lead her, sick as she was, to the door, preceded by a silver and ivory case in which the Body of the Saint of saints was kept with great devotion. Prostrating herself before the

Convent of San Damiano
in Assisi

St. Clare and the Assault on Assisi, Giuseppe Cesari
(1568-1640). Hermitage Museum, St. Petersburg

Enrico de Vroom (1587),
Miracle of St. Clare

Urn containing the body of
St. Clare, Assisi

Painting of the
Miracle of St. Clare

St. Clare, detail of
the great Cross of
Gianfrancesco dalle
Croci

St. Clare and the Saracens.
Painting by Piero
Casentini. Holy Cross
Monastery, Pignataro
Maggiore

Lord, she spoke tearfully to her Christ: 'Behold, my Lord, is it possible that You wish to deliver these Your defenseless handmaids, whom I have taught for love for You, into the hands of pagans? I pray You, Lord, protect these Your handmaids whom I cannot save alone.' Suddenly a voice like that of a child resounded in her ears from the tabernacle: *'I will always protect you!'* 'My Lord,' she added, 'if it is Your will, protect also this city which sustains us for love of You.' Christ replied, *'It will have to undergo trials, but it will be defended by My protection.'* Then the virgin, raising a face bathed in tears, comforted her weeping sisters: 'I assure you, daughters, that you will suffer no harm; only have faith in Christ.' There was no delay; the fierce Saracens were immediately filled with fear and fled back over the walls they had scaled, unnerved by the strength of her who prayed. And Clare immediately admonished those who had heard the voice I spoke of above, telling them severely: 'Take care not to tell anyone about that voice while I am still alive, dearest daughters.'"

ST. FAUSTINA KOWALSKA

POLAND, 20TH CENTURY

The most recent practice linked to devotion to the Sacred Heart of Jesus is veneration of the image of Divine Mercy, which comes from the apparitions of Jesus to the Polish nun, St. Faustina Kowalska. Jesus appeared to her on February 22, 1931, with His right hand raised in blessing and His left hand pointing towards His Sacred Heart, which emitted two rays: one pale, the other bright red. These rays represent the Blood and Water which flowed from Jesus' pierced side while on the Cross. They symbolize the purifying power of Baptism and Confession and the regenerative power of the Holy Eucharist.

Jesus said to St. Faustina: "I desire that this image be venerated... throughout the world. I promise that the soul that will venerate this image will not perish. I also promise victory over [its] enemies already here on earth, especially at the hour of death. I Myself will defend it as My own glory." (*Diary* #47, #48)

Jesus Himself explained the significance of this devotion: "Tell [all people], My daughter, that I am Love and Mercy itself. Souls who spread the honor of My mercy I shield through their entire life as a tender mother her infant....Tell aching mankind to snuggle close to My merciful Heart, and I will fill it with peace." (*Diary* #1074, #1075)

"Souls perish in spite of My bitter Passion. I am giving them the last hope of salvation; that is, the Feast of My Mercy.... [My unfathomable Mercy] is a sign for the end times; after it will come the day of justice. (*Diary* #965, #848)

At the same time as He manifested His Infinite Mercy, the Lord also showed St. Faustina hell. "Today, I was led by an Angel to the chasms of hell. It is a place of great torture; how awesomely large and extensive it is! The kinds of tortures I saw: the first torture that constitutes hell is the loss of God; the

"My daughter, write down these words: All those souls who will glorify My mercy and spread its worship, encouraging others to trust in My mercy, will not experience terror at the hour of death. My mercy will shield them in that final battle.... My daughter, encourage souls to say the chaplet which I have given to you. It pleases Me to grant everything they ask of Me by saying the chaplet." (Diary #1540, #1541)

second is perpetual remorse of conscience; the third is that one's condition will never change; the fourth is the fire that will penetrate the soul without destroying it—a terrible suffering, since it is a purely spiritual fire, lit by God's anger; the fifth torture is continual darkness and a terrible suffocating smell, and despite the darkness, the devils and the souls of the damned see each other and all the evil, both of others and their own; the sixth torture is the constant company of Satan; the seventh torture is horrible despair, hatred of God, vile words, curses and blasphemies....

"Let the sinner know that he will be tortured throughout all eternity.... I am writing this at the command of God, so that no soul may find an excuse by saying there is no hell, or that nobody has ever been there, and so no one can say what it is like.... What I have written is but a pale shadow of the things I saw." *(Diary #741)*

Quotations from St. Faustina's writings are taken from the *Diary of St. Maria Faustina Kowalska: Divine Mercy in My Soul* © 1987 Congregation of Marians of the Immaculate Conception, Stockbridge, MA 01263 www.marian.org. Used with permission.

"Tell everyone,
My daughter,
that I am Love
and Mercy itself."

the Divine Mercy

DIVINE MERCY CHAPLET

Jesus said to St. Faustina: "This prayer will serve to appease My wrath. You will recite it for 9 days, on the beads of the rosary, in the following manner:

First of all, you will say one OUR FATHER and HAIL MARY and the I BELIEVE IN GOD.

Then on the OUR FATHER beads, you will say the following words:
Eternal Father, I offer You the Body and Blood, Soul and Divinity of Your dearly beloved Son, Our Lord Jesus Christ, in atonement for our sins and those of the whole world.

On the HAIL MARY beads you will say the following words:
For the sake of His Sorrowful Passion, have mercy on us and on the whole world.

In conclusion, three times you will recite these words:
Holy God, Holy Mighty One, Holy Immortal One, have mercy on us and on the whole world." (Diary #476)

In the year 2000 John Paul II instituted the liturgical feast of Divine Mercy, which is celebrated each year on the Sunday after Easter.

Św. Faustyna

Jesus said to St. Faustina: "My daughter, help me to save a certain dying sinner. Say the chaplet that I have taught you for him." She wrote: "When I began to say the chaplet, I saw the man dying in the midst of terrible torment and struggle. His Guardian Angel was defending him, but he was, as it were, powerless against the enormity of the soul's misery. A multitude of devils was waiting for the soul. But while I was saying the chaplet, I saw Jesus just as He is depicted in the image. The rays which issued from Jesus' Heart enveloped the sick man, and the powers of darkness fled in panic. The sick man peacefully breathed his last. When I came to myself, I understood how very important the chaplet was for the dying. It appeases the anger of God." *(Diary 1565)*

St. Faustina wrote that "during Holy Mass, when the Lord Jesus was exposed in the Blessed Sacrament, before Holy Communion, I saw two rays coming out from the Blessed Host, just as they are painted in the image, one of them red and the other pale." *(Diary # 336)*

Shrine of the Divine Mercy in Krakow, Poland

ST. FRANCIS OF ASSISI

ITALY, 13TH CENTURY

St. Francis had a particular affection for lambs, to whom Jesus Christ is often compared in the Sacred Scriptures because of His sweetness and gentle nature.

St. Francis of Assisi, Giotto

*T*he Franciscan historical chronicles tell us that "during a visit to Rome, the saint kept with him a little lamb, inspired by his devotion to Christ, his most beloved Lamb. Upon his departure, he entrusted it to a noble matron, Lady Jacopa dei Sette Soli, to keep in her home. The lamb, as if spiritually educated by the saint in matters of the soul, never left the woman's side, whether she went to church, remained in church, or returned from church. Some mornings, if the lady was late in awakening, the lamb would jump up and nudge her with his little horns, and wake her with his bleats, encouraging her by his gestures and expressions to hurry to church. Because of this, the lady admired and loved that lamb, disciple of Francis and teacher of devotion. [...]

"One day while walking on the outskirts of Siena, Saint Francis encountered a large herd of grazing sheep. As he always did, he greeted them kindly, and they, having stopped grazing, all ran towards him, raising their heads and meeting his gaze. They greeted him with such joy that the brothers

Upper Basilica of St. Francis, Assisi

St. Francis, Francisco Ribalta Museum of Prado, Madrid

J. Van Eyck, *The Mystical Lamb*

Portrait of St. Francis, Speco

and shepherds were amazed, seeing the lambs and even the rams jumping around in such a wondrous way. [...]

"Another time, at the Portiuncula, some people brought a lamb as a gift to this man of God, and he accepted it with gratitude, because he loved the innocence and simplicity that sheep demonstrate by nature. The man of God admonished the little lamb to praise God and absolutely not to bother the brothers. The lamb, for her part, seemed to sense the piety of this man of God, and put these teachings into practice with great care. When she heard the brothers singing in the choir, she would enter the church, bend her knees, and emit tender harmonious bleats in front of the altar of the Virgin Mother of the Lamb, as if desirous of greeting her. During the celebration of the Mass, at the moment of the Elevation, she would bow down, knees bent, as if this devout little animal wished to reproach men of little faith for their irreverence and encourage devout men in their reverence towards the Blessed Sacrament."

ST. GERMAINE COUSIN

To attend Mass, St. Germaine Cousin (1579-1601) had to cross a raging stream; the waters parted and let her pass without hindrance.

Painting depicting the miracle

When this young shepherd girl's mother died, her father married a woman who, from the very start, was hostile towards her because Germaine's face was disfigured by acne. The stepmother, who could not stand the sight of Germaine, convinced her husband to have Germaine live in the basement under the steps. The poor girl found herself so completely isolated in that basement that the mice were often her only companions.

Germaine, however, was very close to the Lord and was particularly devoted to the Blessed Sacrament, which she received daily. Every day she would leave her sheep unattended to receive the Holy Eucharist, and miraculously the herd was never attacked by wolves.

To reach the church, however, Germaine had to cross a stream called Courbet. One day heavy rain made the stream impossible to cross, but the young girl courageously decided to try anyway so she could receive Communion. Before stepping into the water, she made the sign of the cross, and as she was reciting her prayers the waters miraculously parted. The same thing happened on her way back as well.

Tomb of St. Germaine

Germaine's stepmother forced her to live in a base-ment under the steps

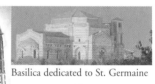

Basilica dedicated to St. Germaine

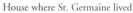

House where St. Germaine lived

Print depicting the miracle of the unattended herd, which was never attacked by wild animals

Charles Martel had committed a grave sin of incest with his sister, and stricken by remorse, decided to go to Provence and present himself to an abbot named Gilles, who was well-known for his holiness, to seek absolution for this sin without actually confessing it and while keeping it a secret. St. Gilles was offering a Mass for the resolution of this situation when an angel appeared and placed himself near the altar, carrying in his hand a book in which the "unconfessable" sin was written. As the celebration continued, the writing in the book faded little by little until it completely disappeared, and Charles Martel found himself absolved.

The Mass of St. Gilles in the Presence of Charles Martel, National Gallery of London

*P*rior to his famous victory over the Saracens at Poitiers, Charles Martel had committed a grave sin against the sixth commandment. Stricken by remorse, he did not dare confess the sin, so vile was the act he had committed. He decided, therefore, to go to Provence and present himself to a well-known abbot of the time named Gilles, in order to seek absolution without actually confessing the sin and while keeping the sin a secret. St. Gilles was officiating at a Mass offered for the resolution of the situation, when an angel appeared and placed himself near the altar, carrying in his hand a book in which the "unconfessable" sin was written. As the celebration continued, the writing in the book faded little by little until it completely disappeared, and Charles Martel found himself absolved.

The story of this sin and its miraculous absolution was so famous that popular fervor often attributed it to Charlemagne, and not to Charles Martel, as if the real participant were not sufficiently authoritative.

St. Gilles was well-known even before he performed this miracle. Originally

St. Gilles and the fawn

Jean-Honoré Gonon, *The Battle of Charles Martel and Abd-er-Rahman, King of the Saracens*

Charles of Steuben, *The Battle of Poitiers*

A window picturing Charles Martel

from Athens, he had retreated to a hermitage in a forest of Gard, France, where a fawn visited him daily to nourish him with her own milk. One day while hunting, the king of the Visigoths followed the animal to the threshold of the grotto where the hermit lived, and shot the fawn. In order to make reparation for the sacrilege he had committed, the king had a great monastery built which was given the name of St. Gilles-du-Gard, and which became an important stop along the pilgrimage route to Compostela before itself becoming a place of pilgrimage. St. Gilles has been invoked for help with difficult confessions.

ST. JULIANA OF LIÈGE

LIÈGE, BELGIUM, 1374

"Even though the Eucharist is solemnly celebrated every day of the year, on one day we pay special honor to the Body of Christ. We may, of course, invoke the Lord with our minds and our spirits at any time, but we do not in this way obtain the Real Presence of Christ. With the Eucharistic commemoration, however, Jesus Christ is actually present with us in His own substance. As the risen Christ told us prior to his Ascension: 'And behold, I am with you always, until the end of the age' (Mt 28:20). ...He would remain and be with them even by his bodily presence" (Pope Urban IV: *Transiturus de hoc mundo).*

Monstrance kept in the Sanctuary of St. Juliana, Liège

St. Juliana of Liège, who lived in 13th-century Belgium, had a vision in which she saw a full moon darkened in one spot. She heard a mysterious heavenly voice state that the moon represented the Church at that time, and the dark spot showed that a great feast in honor of Corpus Christi was missing from the liturgical calendar. She reported this vision to the local ecclesiastical authority, the Archdeacon of Liège, Jacques Pantéléon, who was later to become Pope Urban IV.

In 1246, the Bishop of Liège, Robert of Thourotte, established within his diocese a feast in honor of the Blessed Sacrament, and it was celebrated for the first time on June 5, 1249. In 1264, Pope Urban IV (the former Archdeacon of Liège, to whom Blessed Juliana reported her vision) issued a papal bull extending the celebration to the universal Church. He also commissioned St. Thomas Aquinas to compose the Office for the Mass and the Liturgy of the Hours for the feast.

St. Juliana

Stained-glass window depicting St. Juliana's vision

ST. MARGARET MARY ALACOQUE
FRANCE, 17TH CENTURY

The message received by the Visitation nun, St. Margaret Mary Alacoque of Paray-le-Monial, contains the "Twelve Promises of the Sacred Heart" in which Jesus reveals the graces linked to this devotion. Love for the Sacred Heart of Jesus is directly related to love for the Eucharist. As the great apostle of this devotion, the Jesuit priest Henri Ramière, wrote, "It is in the Eucharist that we truly find the Heart of Jesus nearest us; it is in the Eucharist that He unites Himself to us in the most intimate way, and we to Him."

St. Claude de la Colombiere

St. Margaret Mary received many mystical gifts and revelations from Jesus.

We list here the "Twelve Promises of the Sacred Heart" which the Lord revealed to her:

1. I will give them all the graces necessary for their state in life. (Letter #141)

2. I will give peace in their families. (Letter #35)

3. I will console them in all their afflictions. (Letter #141)

4. They shall find in My Heart a secure refuge during life and especially at the hour of death. (Letter #141)

5. I will pour abundant blessings on all their undertakings. (Letter #141)

6. Sinners shall find in My Heart the source and infinite ocean of mercy. (Letter #132)

7. Tepid souls shall become fervent. (Letter #132)

8. Fervent souls shall speedily rise to great perfection. (Letter #132)

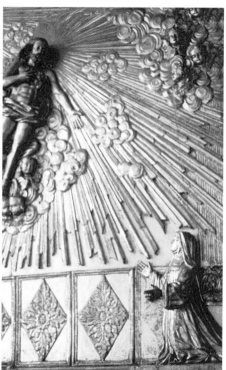

9. I will bless the homes in which the image of My Sacred Heart shall be displayed and venerated. (Letter #35)

10. I will give to priests the power to touch the most hardened hearts. (Letter #141)

11. Those who propagate this devotion shall have their names written in My Heart, never to be blotted out. (Letter #141)

12. The all-powerful love of My Heart will grant to all those who shall receive Communion on the first Fridays of nine consecutive months the grace of final repentance; they shall not die under My displeasure, nor without receiving the Sacraments; My Heart shall be their assured refuge at the last hour. (Letter #86)

St. Margaret Mary received many mystical gifts and revelations from Jesus.

"The Church, true minister of the Blood of Redemption, was born from the pierced Heart of the Redeemer, and from that same heart also comes the grace of the sacraments in superabundance, which instills eternal life in the children of the Church." Pope Pius XII

"Jesus is found in the sacrament of the Eucharist, in which love keeps Him bound like a victim, always ready to be sacrificed for the glory of His Father and for our salvation. His life is totally hidden from the eyes of the world, which succeed in seeing only the poor and humble appearances of bread and wine. [...] Jesus is always alone in the Blessed Sacrament. Try never to miss a single Communion, because we could give no greater joy to our enemy the devil!"

A design by St. Margaret Mary

"We desire that all those who actively labor to establish the Kingdom of Jesus in the world, take devotion to the Sacred Heart of Jesus as their banner. [...] Ardently wishing to offer a secure barrier against the impious plottings of the enemies of God and of the Church, and to have families and nations return to the love of God and neighbor, we do not hesitate to propose devotion to the Sacred Heart of Jesus as the most efficacious school of divine charity, on which charity it is necessary to construct the Kingdom of God in the souls of individuals, in domestic society and among the nations." (Pope Pius XII, *Haurietis aquas, 82-83*)

"The Church wishes to incite the faithful ever more to draw near with confidence to this Holy Mystery and to consume more and more hearts in the flames of that divine love with which the Sacred Heart burned when, in His infinite love, He instituted the Most Holy Eucharist." Pope Benedict XV

THE SERVANT OF GOD
MARTHE ROBIN
FRANCE, 1902-1981

The French philosopher Jean Guitton left us a powerful testimony regarding Marthe Robin: "She was a peasant of the French countryside, who for thirty years has taken neither food nor drink, living on the Eucharist alone, reliving the pains of the Passion of Jesus every Friday through her stigmata. A woman who was perhaps the most unusual, the most extraordinary and disconcerting person of our age, but who even in the age of television remained unknown to the public, buried in profound silence... From our very first meeting, I understood that Marthe Robin would be a 'sister in charity,' always, as she was for thousands of visitors."

Jesus said to Marthe when she was in a state of ecstasy: "My priests, my priests, give everything for them. My Mother and I love them very much. Give me all your sufferings, everything you are suffering at this moment, everything in which my Love wants to submerge you. Give me your isolation and your solitude, the solitude in which I place you, all without reservation for my priests. Offer yourself to the Father with me, for them; don't be afraid for having to suffer too much for my priests; they have a pressing need for those things that I am about to do through you for their advantage."

Marthe Robin was born on March 13, 1902, in Châteauneuf-de-Galaure (Drôme), in France, to a family of peasants, and spent her entire life in her parents' home, where she died February 6, 1981. Marthe's entire existence revolved around Jesus in the Eucharist, Who for her was "the One who heals, consoles, sustains, and blesses—my *Everything*."

In 1928, after a serious neurological illness, Marthe found herself almost completely paralyzed. It was especially hard for her to swallow, because those particular muscles had been affected. Moreover, due to an eye condition, she was forced to live in almost absolute darkness. According to her spiritual director, Fr. Finet: "When she received the stigmata in early October 1930, Marthe had already experienced the pains of the Passion since 1925, the year she offered herself as a victim of love. That day, Jesus said she was chosen, next to the Blessed Virgin, to live the Passion more intensely. No one else would experience it so completely. He added that each day she would suffer more, and at night she would no longer be able to sleep. After the stigmata,

The house where Marthe lived her whole life, Châteauneuf-de-Galaure, Drôme (France)

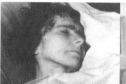

Marthe received the gift of the stigmata from the Lord. Beginning in 1930, every Thursday evening she relived the suffering of Jesus at Gethsemane

Father Finet, Marthe's spiritual director and founder of the "Foyers of Charity"

Marthe was neither able to eat nor drink. The ecstasy lasted until Monday or Tuesday."

Marthe Robin accepted all these sufferings out of love for Jesus the Redeemer and for the sinners He wanted to save.

In fact, beyond the extraordinary mystical phenomena, extremely significant was the work of evangelization Marthe managed to accomplish, despite her condition, thanks to the help of Father Finet, with whom she founded sixty "Foyers of Charity" (centers or homes of light, charity and love) throughout the world.

In Belgium, at Bois-d'Haine, the Servant of God Anne-Louise Lateau lived for twelve years without eating or drinking and without sleeping, starting on March 26, 1871. On January 11, 1868, she received the stigmata on her feet, hands, head, chest, and right shoulder. She lived thus until the end of her life. On April 23, 1873, Pope Leo XIII made the following declaration regarding Anne-Louise's case, "The Bois-d'Haine event is an extraordinary one. You can affirm on my behalf that medical science will never be able to explain such a fact." Anne-Louise died on August 25, 1883, at age 33. In 1991 the cause for her beatification was officially opened.

ST. MARY OF EGYPT

EGYPT, SIXTH CENTURY

This Eucharistic miracle took place in the life of St. Mary of Egypt, who lived in the desert for 47 years. The account of her life was written by Bishop Sophronius of Jerusalem in the 6th century. St. Mary walked across the Jordan River to receive Communion from the monk Zosimus.

We are told that when St. Mary was 12 years old she ran away from her parents and went to Alexandria. There she led a very dissolute life for 16 years. One day she came upon a ship about to set sail with an odd-looking group of passengers. She inquired who they might be and where they were going. Mary was told that they were pilgrims sailing toward Jerusalem for the feast of the Exaltation of the Cross. She decided to join them. Once at their destination, she tried to enter the church on the feast day, but she was held back at the door by a mysterious force. Fearfully she raised her eyes to an image of the Holy Virgin and was overcome with deep sorrow for the sinful life she had led until that day. Only then was she able to make her way into the church and worship the True Cross.

She did not remain long in Jerusalem. "If you go across the Jordan, you will find peace," Our Lady had said to her. The following day, after her confession and Communion, Mary made her way across the Jordan to the Arabian Desert. There she lived for 47 years in solitude, encountering neither man nor beast. Her skin shriveled, her hair grew long and turned white, but the promise of the Virgin proved true;

Jordan River

St. Mary of Egypt, Diocesan
Museum of Milan

Emile Nolde, *Death in the Desert*

Marcantonio Franceschini, *Last Communion of
St. Mary of Egypt* (1690)

in that inhospitable desert she found peace of soul.

One day she met the monk Zosimus and asked him to come back in a year and bring her Communion. A year later, as he had promised, Zosimus came to the bank of the Jordan River with the Eucharist, but Mary did not appear. In great sorrow Zosimus prayed: "Lord, my God, King and Creator of all, do not deprive me of my desire, but grant that I may see this Your most holy servant." Then he thought, "Now what will I do if she appears? There is no boat around to get me across. I will not achieve my wish." As he thought this, Mary appeared on the opposite shore, and Zosimus rejoiced and praised God. Then he saw her make the sign of the Cross over the water and walk out on it as though it were dry land!

When another year had passed Zosimus returned, but this time all he found were the mummified remains of the saintly penitent. A lion helped him dig her grave and bury the body.

BL. NIELS STEENSEN

After a youth spent in study and then in scientific research, Niels Steensen, at age 28, while watching a Corpus Christi procession, converted to the Catholic Church as he recognized the greatness and magnificence of the Eucharist, the Real Presence of Jesus in the Host. He then decided to become a priest and missionary in his own country.

Portrait of Bl. Nicholas Steenson

Niels Steensen was born in Copenhagen, Denmark, on January 1, 1638. From his youth, he was so immersed in the natural sciences that he was considered among the founding fathers of geology, paleontology and crystallography. His prolific scientific activity led him to travel all over Europe.

On June 24, 1666, in Livorno, Italy, Niels received the grace of conversion to the Catholic faith. His biographers wrote, "He observed with curiosity and perplexity the Corpus Christi procession and the fervor surrounding it. The large *Piazza d'Armi* was bursting with colors and sounds. A loud, prolonged ringing of bells could be heard.

The young man was recalling another procession he had watched three years before in Louvain, Belgium, where many students were lined up and dozens of black-robed professors were walking. He could perceive something different here. Maybe it was a sense of joy, a new human warmth... or maybe his eyes had changed? Long lines of men in white tunics passed him, singing. Banners and tapestries were swinging in the gentle breeze coming from the sea. Friars and priests were processing too, dressed in their white surplices adorned with lace and tassels. Even more priests were part of the procession, wearing their copes shining in the sun, and children holding censers. Finally, a big golden canopy passed by, and

NICOLAVS STENONIVS

under it a minister of the Church, solemnly dressed, absorbed in his thoughts, pressing to his heart the precious monstrance with the Sacred Host…. People knelt as the Blessed Sacrament passed by, and eyes shone with love as they gazed upon the Host, all heads bowed in adoration. Petals and flowers rained down on all sides.

"The young Niels Steensen spent the whole day with great uneasiness in his heart. He remembered the Jesuit priest in Paris with whom he had discussed the Real Presence of Jesus in the consecrated Bread. The Jesuit priest had emphasized the meaning of Jesus' words at the Last Supper, 'This is my Body,' and then St.

Paul's First Letter to the Corinthians. That day Niels Steensen decided to convert to Catholicism. He immediately entered the seminary, and after nine years of study was ordained a priest. He described his conversion: 'As soon as I attentively pondered God's favors to me, they seemed so immense that I could do nothing but offer Him the best of myself and in the best way possible, from the bottom of my heart… Therefore, having come to know the great dignity of the priesthood… I asked and obtained the favor that I, too, might offer the Immaculate Host to the Eternal Father for myself and others.'"

ST. SATYRUS

4TH CENTURY

In his work, *De excessu fratris Satyri*, St. Ambrose himself describes this Eucharistic miracle involving his brother Satyrus. St. Satyrus was saved from a shipwreck thanks to the Eucharist.

St. Satyrus and the Eucharist

St. Ambrose writes of his brother Satyrus: "What shall I say of his observance of the worship of God? One episode will suffice. Before being fully initiated into the sublime mysteries (First Communion), he experienced a shipwreck. When his ship ran aground on some reefs, and while, all around, the waves were tearing it apart, he was not afraid of dying but of having to leave this life without having been nourished by the Sacred Mysteries. So he asked for the Eucharist from those whom he knew to be initiated into the Divine Sacrament and placed the Holy Eucharist in a handkerchief, which he hung around his neck. Then he threw himself into the sea and looked for a plank loosened from the hulk of the ship to hang onto, but did not try to swim away to save himself, because he had put his trust only in the weapons of the faith. Since he was convinced that he was sufficiently protected and defended by this faith, he did not look for any other help.

"Then, as soon as he was saved from the waves and reached land, he paid tribute to the Captain to whom he had entrusted himself. As soon as he was saved and realized that all

his servants had also been saved, he went to the church of God, without complaining about the goods he had lost, to thank Him for having saved him and to get to know His *Eternal Mysteries.* He said there was no more important duty than that of giving thanks... He who had experienced the great help of the *Heavenly Mysteries* wrapped in a handkerchief, considered it a great honor to receive the Holy Eucharist and welcome Christ into the depths of his heart."

ST. STANISLAUS KOSTKA

POLAND, 1550-1568

St. Stanislaus Kostka, at the age of seventeen, fell so gravely ill that he seemed very close to death. At the time, he was living in the home of a Protestant nobleman who would not even permit a Catholic priest to visit him. Stanislaus was not discouraged, and one night, in the presence of his tutor, he received Communion in a miraculous way. A few days later he recovered and decided to enter the Jesuit Order.

Tomb of St. Stanislaus, St. Andrew's Church at the Quirinal, Rome

$\mathcal{S}$t. Stanislaus Kostka was born in 1550 in Rostkow, a few miles from Warsaw. In 1564, at the age of fourteen, Stanislaus was sent to Vienna with his older brother to complete his studies with the Jesuits. He liked his studies and the orderly life at the college very much, and considered dedicating himself to the religious life. Unfortunately the Jesuits had to close the college, and Stanislaus, along with his brother and their tutor, were forced to leave, accepting the hospitality of a Lutheran nobleman. Stanislaus maintained exemplary religious behavior in spite of pressure from his brother, tutor, and host, who all criticized him.

Stanislaus accepted it all with patience and submission, even praying for them during the night.

At about the age of seventeen, Stanislaus became gravely ill. He belonged to the Fraternity of St. Barbara, whose members trust their patroness to grant them the grace of Communion at the point of death. In this Stanislaus had total faith. One night he awakened his tutor, who was keeping watch beside him, exclaiming: "Here is St. Barbara! Here she is, with two angels! She's bringing me the Blessed Sacrament!" And so it was; the angels inclined towards him and gave him Holy Communion. The

St. Barbara

St. Stanislaus Receives Holy Communion from an Angel, Diocesan Museum of Milan

young man, serene, lay back on his bed.

A few days later, to everyone's surprise, Stanislaus awoke perfectly healed, declaring that he wanted to go personally to thank the Lord and expressing his desire to become a religious. The Jesuit regional superior rejected him because of his young age and because his father had not given permission, but Stanislaus did not lose heart. He decided to immediately try again in Germany or even in Italy. He removed his fine clothes, dressed like a peasant, and walked towards Augusta where the great St. Peter Canisius, provincial of the Jesuits in Germany, resided.

Noticing Stanislaus' absence, his brother searched for him and began to feel remorse for his hostile conduct. Meanwhile, St. Peter Canisius carefully evaluated the young man's vocation and decided to send him to the Jesuit seminary in Rome. In his letter of recommendation, St. Peter Canisius wrote: "Stanislaus, a noble Pole, a just man full of zeal, was tested for a certain time at the college in Dillingen, and showed himself ever exact in his duty and firm in his vocation... We hope and expect great things from him."

TERESA NEUMANN

GERMANY, 1898 - 1962

Teresa Neumann's life changed radically after her miraculous recovery from paralysis and total blindness at the age of 25. A few years later, she received the stigmata and began the fast which lasted 36 years until her death. Her only nourishment was the Holy Eucharist, and for this reason the Nazi authorities, during World War II, withdrew her food ration card and gave her a double ration of soap to wash her laundry, because every Friday she was drenched in blood while in ecstasy, experiencing the Passion of Christ. Hitler was very fearful of Teresa and ordered that no one should harm her.

Teresa Neumann was born in Konnersreuth, Germany, on April 8th, 1898, to an extremely poor Catholic family. As she wrote in her diaries, her greatest ambition was to become a missionary in Africa, but this was not possible as she was a victim of an accident at the age of 20. In 1918 a terrible fire broke out in a nearby factory, and Teresa immediately ran to help. In the process of passing buckets of water to extinguish the flames, she incurred a severe lesion of the spinal cord which caused complete blindness and paralysis in both legs.

Teresa then passed her days in prayer, but one day she was miraculously healed in the presence of Fr. Naber, who wrote: "Teresa described a vision of a great light and an extraordinarily sweet voice asking her whether she wished to be healed. Teresa's surprising answer was that it would not make any difference to her whether she would be healed, stay the way she was or even die, as long as it was the will of God. The mysterious voice told her that 'that very day she would receive a small joy, the healing of her infirmities, but that she would still have much suffering to endure in her future.'"

For a while, Teresa enjoyed good health, but in 1926 her important mystical experiences began. These were to last

The house where Teresa was born

Teresa's tomb at Konnersreuth

Teresa's parish

Teresa dies at Konnersreuth in 1962

Teresa at 4 years old

Teresa after her illness

Teresa receiving Holy Communion on Easter Sunday 1934

Teresa Neumann: stigmata on heart and hands (medical photograph, 1926)

until the day she died. She received the stigmata and began a complete fast with the Eucharist as her only nourishment. Fr. Naber, who brought Communion to Teresa every day until her death, wrote: "In her, God's promised word is literally accomplished: 'My Flesh is real food and my Blood is true drink.'" Teresa offered the Lord her physical sufferings, which were due to the loss of blood caused by the stigmata which began every Thursday, the day when Jesus' Passion started, and lasted until Sunday, the day of His Resurrection. These sufferings were offered in intercession for sinners who asked her help. Every time she was called to a person's deathbed, she also witnessed that soul's judgment, which takes place immediately after death.

Ecclesiastical authorities carried out many investigations of Teresa's continuous fasting. Carl Strater, S.J., assigned by the Bishop of Ratisbonne to study the life of the stigmatic, confirmed: "The significance of Teresa Neumann's fast is to show the whole world the value of the Eucharist, to help the world understand that Christ is actually present under the species of bread and that the Eucharist can preserve even physical life."

ST. THOMAS AQUINAS

During the years of his mature theological thought, from 1269 to 1272, St. Thomas Aquinas was called to Paris to resolve the complicated question of the nature of the Eucharist. Before St. Thomas started his dissertation, he went to the church to pray, and then wrote his text. When he had finished, St. Thomas returned to the church, and it was then that Jesus appeared to him to confirm that "you have written well of Me, Thomas."

*D*uring his second term as professor in Paris, St. Thomas found himself in the midst of a dispute among the professors at the Sorbonne regarding the Sacrament of the Eucharist. On the one hand, the senses perceive the presence of the so-called "accidents," such as color, taste, durability, quantity, and extension. But on the other hand, faith confirms that the Body and Blood of Christ are present in the Sacrament, which is an apparent contradiction. Parisian theologians were sharply divided between objective perception by the senses and the value of faith. They decided to ask St. Thomas because they had already seen his philosophical

intelligence and his holiness on more than one occasion. They asked him to pronounce judgment on the matter, agreeing that his theological conclusion would be theirs as well. To this end they wrote down their opposing opinions and gave them to Thomas.

Thomas immediately had recourse to prayer and contemplation, "and as usual, began to pray with great devotion. Then he quickly jotted down, in the briefest and clearest possible way, what his mind discovered and what God inspired."

He returned to the church, and going up to the altar, laid his written answers

G. Francesco Barbieri, called Guercino, *St. Thomas Aquinas Writing Assisted by Angels* (1662)

Miraculous painting in which the crucified Christ came to life and praised St. Thomas' writings (Naples)

Church of St. Dominic in Naples, Italy

there under the gaze of the Crucified Christ and prayed: "Lord Jesus, truly and wonderfully present in this Sacrament, I seek to understand Your truth and teach it without error. So I beseech You, O Lord, to grant me this grace: If the things I have written about You and with Your help are true, make it possible for me to teach them publicly. If, instead, I have written something that is not in accord with revealed truth and alien to the mystery of the Sacrament, keep me from teaching anything that could deviate from the Catholic faith." This was the humble prayer of a theologian who understood that he was dealing with things above him and that

he had a grave responsibility towards his students.

Fr. Reginald, his secretary, and other brethren were fortunate enough to observe St. Thomas deep in prayer. Suddenly Christ appeared and motioned towards his writings, saying: "You wrote well about the sacrament of my Body; you have also resolved, in accord with the truth, the question posed to you, as far as it is possible for man to understand and define these things while still here on earth." Thomas, full of joy and gratitude, prostrated himself in prayer before the Lord.

Young Miguel-Juan Pellicer had had his leg amputated due to an accident. Thanks to his great devotion toward the Blessed Sacrament and the Virgin of Pilar, a great miracle took place which was immediately recognized and approved by the Archbishop of Saragossa who presided over the canonical process. In his final opinion, he wrote that "Miguel-Juan Pellicer of Calanda was miraculously given back his right leg, which had been amputated years before, and this was not a natural occurrence but a miraculous one."

Painting at the Shrine of Pilar depicting the miracle

Miguel-Juan Pellicer was born in 1617 to a poor family of farmers in Calanda, a village about 60 miles from Saragossa. At 19 years of age, he decided to go to work for an uncle near Castellon de la Plata. One day, while working in the fields, he fell under a wagon full of grain and the wheels fractured his right leg. Miguel-Juan was immediately taken to the general hospital in Valencia. Realizing that the doctors could not cure him, he decided to discharge himself and begin a 190-mile trip towards Saragossa to ask Our Lady of Pilar for help. He walked with crutches, leaning the knee of the fractured and now-infected leg on a piece of wood. He reached Saragossa in October 1637, waning and feverish. He dragged himself to the Shrine of Pilar, where he made his confession and received the Holy Eucharist. He was immediately sent to the Royal Hospital of Grace. Given his progressed gangrene, the doctors saw that the only way to save his life was to amputate the leg, so the limb was cut off with a saw and scalpel slightly below the knee and cauterized with red-hot irons.

A young practitioner, Juan Lorenzo Garcia, took the amputated limb and buried it in the cemetery next to the

According to legend, the first chapel of the sanctuary was built by St. James the Great around the year 40, in memory of the miraculous "coming" of the Virgin from Jerusalem to Saragossa in order to comfort the apostle who was completely disillusioned by the poor results of his preaching. The "Pilar" is in fact the alabaster column on which the Virgin's feet rested.

Original document notarized by Miguel Andreu on April 2, 1640, certifying the miracle of Calanda

Pope Pius XII praying before the statue of the Virgin of Pilar that he received as a gift

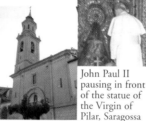

Shrine of the Virgin of Pilar, Saragossa

John Paul II pausing in front of the statue of the Virgin of Pilar, Saragossa

hospital. From that moment, Miguel-Juan was forced to beg for his livelihood near the Shrine of the Virgin of Pilar. Every morning he went to Mass and prayed fervently before the Blessed Sacrament. It was customary for him to rub his mutilated leg with oil from the sanctuary lamp.

After more than three years away from home, he decided to return to his family, who lovingly welcomed him back. In March of 1640, after a vigil in honor of the Virgin, Miguel-Juan, feeling very tired, went to rest earlier than usual and as he always did, he rubbed his wound with oil from the sanctuary lamp from the Shrine of Our Lady of Pilar. When his mother went to check on her son, she saw him sleeping, and noticed that from beneath the blanket stuck out not one, but two feet! Miguel-Juan had miraculously recovered his lost limb, which had been buried three years previously by the practitioner Mr. Garcia. According to the eyewitnesses and to the canonical process, "the leg was pale, smaller in size and muscle mass, but perfectly alive, and allowed him to walk."

THE ANGEL OF PEACE

PORTUGAL, 1916

An angel appeared three times to the shepherds of Fatima to prepare them for the future apparitions of Our Lady and elevate them to a supernatural state with Holy Communion. During the third apparition, the angel gave Lucia a Host from which drops of Blood were falling into the chalice. Francisco and Jacinta, not having yet made their First Holy Communion, were given the contents of the chalice. In this apparition the angel said to them: "Eat and drink the Body and Blood of Jesus Christ, horribly outraged by ungrateful men. Offer reparation for their sins and console your God."

First Apparition of the Angel

"We began to see, in the distance, a light whiter than snow in the form of a young man, quite transparent, and as brilliant as crystal in the rays of the sun. As he came near we were able to see his features: a young man about 14 or 15 years old and very beautiful. We were surprised and quite taken aback. We did not say a word. He reached us and said: 'Do not be afraid. I am the angel of peace. Pray with me.' He knelt, bending his forehead to the ground. With a supernatural impulse we did the same, repeating the words we heard him say: 'My God, I believe, I adore, I hope, and I love You. I ask pardon for those who do not believe, do not adore, do not hope, and do not love You.'

"Then arising, he said, 'Pray in this way. The hearts of Jesus and Mary are attentive to your prayers.' And he disappeared. The supernatural atmosphere that he left us in was so intense we were for a long time unaware of our own existence...."

Second Apparition of the Angel

"The angel said to us: 'What are you doing? You must pray! Pray very much! The hearts of Jesus and Mary have merciful designs on you. You must constantly offer your prayers and sacrifices to God, the Most High.'

Francisco, who did not hear the angel speak, nor was Mary to speak to him in the future, asked Lucia: "The angel gave you Holy Communion, but to Jacinta and me what did he give?" "It was Holy Communion," replied Jacinta with unspeakable happiness. "Did you not see the Blood falling from the Host?" "I felt God in me, but I did not know how it was!" replied Francisco. And kneeling on the ground, he stayed a long time with his sister repeating the prayer of the angel: "Holy Trinity," etc. Among all of the apparitions from Heaven with which he was favored, this was certainly the one that most influenced the good soul of Francisco. The words of the angel asking us to console God, saddened by abuses and sins, deeply impressed his sensitive heart. From that point on, his ideal was to console Our Lord. While Jacinta became the apostle for sinners, Francisco wanted to be the consoler of Christ.

"'How are we to make sacrifices?' I asked.

"'In every possible way, offer sacrifice to God in reparation for the sins by which He is offended, and in supplication for the conversion of sinners. In this way you will bring peace to your country. I am the Guardian Angel of Portugal. Above all, bear and accept with submission the sufferings God will send you.' And he disappeared... These words of the angel cut into our spirits like a light, making us understand who God is, how He loves us, and how He wants us to love Him; the value of sacrifice and how it pleases Him; and how sacrifice can convert sinners."

"We began to see, in the distance, a light whiter than snow in the form of a young man, quite transparent, and brilliant as crystal in the rays of the sun."

Third Apparition of the Angel

"We saw the angel holding in his left hand a chalice, and suspended in the air above it was a Host from which drops of Blood fell into the chalice. Leaving the chalice and the Host suspended in the air, he prostrated himself near us and repeated three times the prayer: *'Most Holy Trinity, Father, Son and Holy Spirit, I adore You profoundly, and I offer You the Most Precious Body, Blood, Soul and Divinity of Jesus Christ, present in all the tabernacles of the world, in reparation for the outrages, sacrileges and indifferences by which He is offended. And by the infinite merits of His Most Sacred Heart and the Immaculate Heart of Mary, I beg the conversion of poor sinners.'* After that he rose and took again in his hands the chalice and the Host. The Host he gave to me, and the contents of the chalice he gave to Jacinta and Francisco, saying at the same time, 'Take and drink the Body and Blood of Jesus Christ, terribly outraged by the ingratitude of men. Offer reparation for their offenses and console your God.' ...Then he disappeared."

Bl. Jacinta Marto reported what Our Lady said during one of the apparitions: "Pray, pray constantly and make sacrifices for sinners. Many souls go to Hell because there is no one to pray and make sacrifices for them..." In addition, "The sins that take most souls to Hell are the sins of the flesh. Certain fashions will be introduced that will offend Jesus very much. People who serve God should not follow the fashions. The Church has no fashions. Jesus is always the same. The sins of the world are very great. If men only knew what eternity is, they would do everything in their power to change their lives. Mankind has lost its way because they do not think of Jesus' death and they do not repent" (cf. CCC 1035).

When Lucia asked Our Lady if she would take them to Heaven, the Virgin replied, "Yes, I will take Jacinta and Francisco soon, but you will stay here for some time. Jesus wants to use you to make me known and loved. He wants to establish in the world devotion to my Immaculate Heart; I promise salvation to all those who practice this devotion. These souls will be dear to God, and like flowers they will be placed by me before his throne."

The angel who appeared to the three shepherds in Fatima in 1916 held in his left hand a chalice and over it, in the air, a Host from which drops of Blood fell into the chalice

After the attempted assasination in St. Peter's Square on May 13, 1981, Pope John Paul II went to Fatima in 1982 in order to thank Our Lady and speak to Sr. Lucia. On March 25, 1984, Pope John Paul II turned in faith to the Virgin of Fatima, making the consecration of the world and Russia.

Photo of the document written by Sr. Lucia and consigned to the Bishop, which describes the third secret revealed to her by Our Lady, which would be publicly announced by Pope John Paul II in the year 2000

Painting depicting the apparition to Sr. Lucia in which Our Lady asked her to spread the reparatory devotion on the five first Saturdays of the month

"We saw the angel holding in his left hand a chalice, and suspended in the air above it was a Host from which drops of Blood fell into the chalice..."

Photo of the crowd gathered around the last apparition of 1917, before the sun began to "dance."

Photograph of the last apparition of October 13, 1917, when the sun began to "dance."

Newspaper article of January 26, 1938, which describes the strange phenomenon of the Northern Lights foretold by Our Lady of Fatima as a sign of the beginning of the war

On October 13, 1917, the pilgrims, numbering 70,000, saw the rain stop suddenly, the clouds open up, and the solar disc become like a silver moon that spun dizzily, similar to a wheel of fire, projecting in every direction beams of multi-colored light, which fantastically lit up the clouds in the sky, the trees, the rocks, the land and the imense crowd. It paused for a few moments and then began again the dance of lights, like a rich and glowing windmill. Again a pause, and then for the third time the fireworks began, more varied and colorful than ever. The crowd had the impression that the sun was falling from the sky and let out a collective scream, "Miracle! Miracle!" When everything was over, even the people's clothes, drenched a short time before, were perfectly dry.

GUADALUPE

MEXICO, 1531

The indisputable historical foundation of the Eucharist is the Incarnation of the Son of God. "Flesh of Christ, flesh of Mary," says St. Augustine. The Church "in Mary contemplates with joy, as in the purest image, what she desires and hopes to be in her entirety" (SC, 103): tabernacle, womb, monstrance. Our Lady appeared in Guadalupe clothed in a dress fastened at the waist with a black belt, identical to those worn by the local women during pregnancy.

Painting depicting Juan Diego and the Virgin

*A*t dawn on December 9, 1531, the young Indian, Juan Diego, went up the hills of Tepeyac, in the northern outskirts of Mexico City, heading towards Tlatelolco, for his usual catechism lesson. Suddenly he heard the sweetest song, and turning towards the source of this sound, he came upon a young woman wearing a radiant dress, who revealed herself as the Virgin Mary. Our Lady requested that Juan Diego ask the Bishop of the capital city to build a temple in the place where she appeared so that all could come to honor her Son Jesus.

Juan Diego obeyed, but Bishop Juan de Zumárraga did not believe him and asked him to ask Mary for a sign. When

the Virgin appeared the third time to Juan Diego, she promised to give him a sign the following day. On Monday, however, he did not go to his appointment because his uncle fell gravely ill and needed to receive the Last Rites. The next day, Juan Diego went out very early directly to Tlatelolco, where he wanted to look for a priest for his uncle. He decided to avoid the hill of Tepeyac so he would not encounter Our Lady, but she met him along the way. He confided his pain to her, and she asked him to have faith in her and told him that his uncle was cured. Then she asked him to go to the top of the hill and collect and bring her the flowers that he would find.

Juan Diego went to the place and found

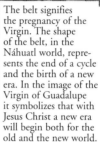

Enlargements of the images present in the eyes of the Virgin

On May 6, 1999 Pope John Paul II before the image of the Virgin of Guadalupe during a pilgrimage

Image of the Virgin which appeared on Juan Diego's cloak

The belt signifies the pregnancy of the Virgin. The shape of the belt, in the Náhuatl world, represents the end of a cycle and the birth of a new era. In the image of the Virgin of Guadalupe it symbolizes that with Jesus Christ a new era will begin both for the old and the new world.

Carlos Salinas and the scientist Tönsmann analyzed and discovered images of the people present during the apparition of Juan Diego in the irises of the eyes of the Virgin of Guadalupe

Here one notes the reflection of the face of Juan Diego

Procession in honor of the Virgin Mary

Image of the Virgin of Guadalupe. Like the Shroud of Turin, it is an image not created by human hands, as scientists J.B. Smith and P.S. Callahan have demonstrated through the analysis of infrared x-rays. Their conclusion is as follows: "The results of the image of Guadalupe are inexplicable."

New shrine at Guadalupe

Old basilica of Guadalupe

it covered with marvelous roses and other flowers, unusual for the winter season and the arid land. He picked the flowers and put them in his tilma, a typical apron worn by the Aztec farmers, and took them to the Virgin. Our Lady told him to go to the Bishop and show him the flowers as proof of the apparition. The man did as he was asked and went to Mexico City where, after a long wait, he was seen by the prelate. Juan Diego showed the Bishop his tilma, and when he opened it, the roses and other flowers fell out, and on the tilma appeared a brilliant image of Our Lady. The Bishop fell to his knees before this miracle. He marveled, and, repenting, asked the Virgin to forgive him for his diffidence. Then he took the tilma and put it in a chapel. The next day Juan Diego returned home anxious to see his uncle, whom he had left gravely ill. Juan Diego found his uncle completely cured. His uncle told him that Our Lady had also appeared to him the day before, presenting herself as Holy Mary of Guadalupe and announcing that he would be cured.

LOURDES

In 1888, a French priest on the National Pilgrimage to Lourdes suggested that a procession with the Blessed Sacrament be held there; a miraculous healing took place. Since then, the sick who come on pilgrimage to Lourdes are always blessed with the Holy Eucharist, and countless cures have taken place during the procession of the Blessed Sacrament. The shrine at Lourdes is a shining example of faith the Real Presence of Jesus in the Eucharist.

Sr. Maria Margherite, cured of an incurable kidney disease during the procession of the Blessed Sacrament

On August 22, 1888, at 4:00 PM, the first procession and blessing of the sick with the Blessed Sacrament took place in Lourdes. It was a priest who first suggested the idea, and since then it has never ceased. On this date in 1888, when the sick were blessed with the Holy Eucharist before the grotto of the apparitions, Pierre Delanoy, who had suffered for many years from ataxia (an inability to coordinate voluntary muscular movements, an illness which inevitably leads to death), was instantly cured when the monstrance passed by him during the procession. This was the first Eucharistic miracle in Lourdes. Since that day, the Eucharistic procession for the sick has always taken place without fail.

Sanctuary of Lourdes

Bernadette's house

Statue of Our Lady in the grotto where she appeared to Bernadette

Pius IX proclaimed the dogma of the Immaculate Conception in 1854

One of the oldest photos of Bernadette by the grotto in 1864

St. Bernadette

Brother Léo Shwager, cured of a serious case of multiple sclerosis during the procession of the Blessed Sacrament

Marie Fabre was cured during the procession of the Blessed Sacrament, of a strong dyspepsia (indigestion) which impeded normal nutrition, causing serious problems with anemia

St. Bernadette embraced religious life and entered the convent of the Sisters of Charity in Nevers

The incorrupt body of St. Bernadette in the motherhouse of the Sisters of Charity in Nevers

Marie-Thérèse Canin was cured of tuberculosis during the procession of the Blessed Sacrament

Marie Bigot, semi-blind and deaf, recovered her hearing and sight during the procession of the Blessed Sacrament

Alice Couteaul, cured of sclerosis during the procession of the Blessed Sacrament

Louise Jamain was cured of pulmonary and intestinal tuberculosis during the procession of the Blessed Sacrament

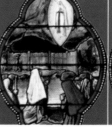

Catherine Labouré was born on May 2, 1806, to a family of farmers. On April 21, 1830, she entered the novitiate of the Daughters of Charity at their motherhouse near Rue du Bac in Paris. Here, in 1830, Catherine had the famous apparition of Mary Immaculate, who told her, "Have a medal struck like this; those who wear it around the neck will receive great graces." During her entire stay at Rue du Bac, Catherine also had the grace of seeing Jesus in the consecrated Host, both at the moment of Holy Communion and during exposition of the Blessed Sacrament.

*C*atherine herself described the moment of the apparition: "While in deep silence at Eucharistic adoration I seemed to hear a sound coming from the side of the tribune, like the rustle of a silk dress. I looked up and saw the Blessed Virgin. She was of medium build and indescribably beautiful. A white veil fell from her head almost to her feet and rested upon a half-globe. Her hands, raised to waist level in a natural position, held another small golden globe with a gold cross on top. Her eyes looked towards Heaven. While I was intent on contemplating her, the Holy Virgin lowered her eyes towards me and said these words: 'This globe that you see represents the entire world, particularly France, and every single person.' And the Virgin added, 'The rays symbolize the graces shed on those who ask me for them,' making me understand how sweet it is to pray to the Holy Virgin and how generous she is to those who invoke her. Then an oval frame formed around the figure of the Holy Virgin, with a semi-circular border of writing in gold above the right hand of Mary spelling out: 'O MARY CONCEIVED WITHOUT SIN, PRAY FOR US WHO HAVE RECOURSE TO THEE.'

Urn containing the body of St. Catherine

Fresco in the church on Rue du Bac showing Catherine with the Virgin Mary

Statue of Mary as she appeared to St. Catherine with the globe, the rays, and the Sacred Heart of Jesus

Image of the Miraculous Medal

Pope John Paul II on a visit to the chapel in the church on Rue du Bac in Paris on May 31, 1980

St. Catherine Labouré

"At this point in the vision, the globe Mary had offered to God disappeared; her hands, full of graces, opened towards the globe upon which her feet rested, crushing the head of a green serpent with yellow spots. Suddenly the frame flipped and I saw the 'back of the medal,' showing the letter 'M' for Mary, surmounted by the Cross, and below the monogram there were two hearts: that of Jesus with the crown of thorns and that of Mary pierced by a sword. Around all this, like a frame, there was a regal crown of twelve little stars.

"Then I heard a voice saying to me, 'Have a medal struck like this. All those who wear this medal, blessed, especially around the neck, and recite this short prayer, will receive the special protection of the Mother of God and will receive great graces. The graces will be abundant for those who wear it with faith.'"

One of St. Jerome's miraculous Communions

St. Bernard Exorcising a Woman with the Blessed Sacrament, Hieron Museum

St. Bonaventure Receiving Communion from the Hand of an Angel, Hieron Museum

St. Secundus, Before Dying, Receiving Holy Communion Brought by a Dove, Hieron Museum

Bl. James of Montieri lived for long periods of time on the Eucharist alone. Jesus Himself gave James Holy Communion on various occasions. An early 16th-century painter depicted one of these miraculous Communions.

St. Juliana Falconieri was always most devoted to the Holy Eucharist. In her last days, a stomach ailment which had afflicted her for a long time, as it became more acute, prevented her from receiving Communion. Before her death in 1341, she asked that a consecrated Host be placed on her chest, and as she recited a prayer, the Host disappeared and left a violet mark, as if the mark had been branded there. She was beatified in 1678 and canonized in 1737.

Bl. Imelda Lambertini, from childhood on, already showed a great love for the Eucharistic Jesus, but the chaplain reminded her that she could only receive Communion when she turned 14. Nevertheless, on May 12, 1333 (the vigil of the Ascension), when she was only 11, she went to Mass and presented herself for Holy Communion. The priest ignored her completely, but the Lord wished to grant little Imelda's desire. A radiant Host rose into the air and stopped in front of her. After she received the Body of Christ, her pure white soul flew straight up to heaven. Bl. Imelda is the patroness of First Communicants.

In earlier times, eight years old was too young to receive the Eucharist, but St. Gerard Magella could not resign himself to this fact and would often weep with such desolation that Heaven itself was moved to pity. One night, St. Michael approached him, placed a white Host on his tongue like the one the priest had refused to give him, and vanished from sight. The following morning, happy and triumphant, Gerard admitted candidly: "The priest refused me Holy Communion, but last night St. Michael the Archangel brought me Holy Communion."

Bl. Emily Bicchieri was the foundress of the Dominican Third Order Regular and always nurtured a great love for the Blessed Sacrament. One day while she was taking care of a fellow Sister who was very sick, she lost track of time and so arrived at the end of the Mass, thus missing Holy Communion. She began to express her regret to the Lord for not having been able to receive Him, and suddenly an angel miraculously appeared to her and gave her Holy Communion.

St. Maria Francesca of the Five Wounds, in the last years of her life, was prevented from participating in the Mass because of a severe illness that left her bedridden. There were many episodes in which some of the priests, especially Fr. Bianchi, saw a Particle of the consecrated large Host and a small amount of the consecrated Wine disappear during their Masses; it was the saint's Guardian Angel who brought her Communion.

One day, St. Lucy Filippini was making her way to Pitigliano, near Grosseto, to inspect a school for craftsmen which she had founded. First, however, she stopped at the church of the Franciscan Fathers to attend Mass. So great was Lucy's desire to receive Jesus in the Eucharist that the Lord wished to reward her with a miracle. When the priest was breaking the large Host in half to place a small Fragment in the chalice, this Fragment flew into the air, radiating light, and came to rest on the tongue of the future saint. Today, the shrine where the miracle took place is under the care of the Filippini Sisters.

At age 22, Bl. Thomas of Cori (1655-1729) entered the Franciscan Order of Friars Minor at the Monastery of the Most Holy Trinity in Orvieto, Italy. In his apostolate, he was distinguished by his exemplary practice of the Christian virtues. Several times during Mass he had various apparitions of the Child Jesus.

This painting represents St. Frances of Rome with some of her companions in ecstatic wonder before the monstrance from which beams of light radiate (Civic Art Museum of Pordenone)

During her stay at Proceno, the Dominican St. Agnes Segni would go into the monastery garden alone to pray near an olive tree. One Sunday morning at the break of dawn she was immersed in prayer, and only several hours later did she realize that it was a feast day and that she was obliged to attend Mass in the monastery choir. However, an angel of the Lord came bearing an immaculate Host, giving her Holy Communion. This incident was repeated on other occasions.

The biographer of St. Clare of Montefalco recounts in the acts for her canonization process that "one day Clare came up to Holy Communion without her mantle. Sr. Giovanna rebuked her harshly, saying, 'Go away — I don't want you to receive Holy Communion.' Hearing these words, Clare realized that she was without her mantle and felt such deep regret that after she returned to her cell, she wept bitterly. While she was praying, amid her tears Christ appeared to her, and embracing her, gave her Holy Communion, leaving her deeply consoled."

Bl. Angela of Foligno recounted that "on one occasion I saw Christ under the guise of a small Child, Who nevertheless appeared great and majestic, like a king. It seemed that, seated on His throne, He held in His hand something like a symbol of authority [...] Then, when the others knelt down, I did not do so, and I don't know if I ran up close to the altar or if I could not move from sheer delight and contemplation, and I experienced great regret that the priest put the Host back on the altar so quickly."

The great mystic St. Teresa of Avila often enjoyed visions of heaven during Holy Mass

One of the miraculous Masses of St. Gregory the Great, in which Christ appeared crucified (Diocesan Museum of Trier)

An extensive assortment of photographs and historical descriptions, this exhibition, sponsored by the Real Presence Eucharistic Education and Adoration Association, Inc., presents some of the principal Eucharistic miracles which have taken place throughout the ages in various countries of the world, and have been recognized by the Church.

By means of 140 laminated panels, one can "virtually visit" the places where the miracles took place.

The exhibition has already visited more than five hundred parishes in Italy and in other countries and has been translated into numerous languages.

The exhibition is comprised of 140 laminated panels (60x80 cm), made to be hung on any surface.

If your parish or organization would like to exhibit the Church-approved photographic Vatican International Exhibition, *The Eucharistic Miracles of the World,* or if you would like more information about the exhibition, please contact:

Real Presence Eucharistic Education and Adoration Association
718 Liberty Lane
Lombard, IL 60148
Phone: 815-254-4420
Email: exhibition@therealpresence.org
Website: www.therealpresence.org